New Cuts
for New Quilts

MORE WAYS TO STACK THE DECK

Karla Alexander

Martingale®
& COMPANY

CREDITS

President: Nancy J. Martin

CEO: Daniel J. Martin

COO: Tom Wierzbicki

Publisher: Jane Hamada

Editorial Director: Mary V. Green

Managing Editor: Tina Cook

Technical Editor: Darra Williamson

Copy Editor: Liz McGehee

Design Director: Stan Green

Illustrator: Robin Strobel

Cover and Text Designer: Regina Girard

Photographer: Brent Kane

MISSION STATEMENT

Dedicated to providing quality products
and service to inspire creativity.

DEDICATION

To my husband, Don Alexander

ACKNOWLEDGMENTS

Writing a book is always an event!
Lots of support from family and friends
makes it all come together.

A special thanks to my family; they always
walk the walk with me when I tackle
enormous projects.

Special thanks also to friends who stop
by with coffee and offers of help—
which I often take advantage of.

Finally, a special thanks to my awesome
editor, Darra Williamson, and to
Martingale & Company.

New Cuts for New Quilts:
More Ways to Stack the Deck
© 2006 by Karla Alexander

Martingale® & COMPANY

That Patchwork Place® is an imprint
of Martingale & Company®.

Martingale & Company
20205 144th Ave. NE
Woodinville, WA 98072-8478 USA
www.martingale-pub.com

Printed in China
11 10 09 08 07 06   8 7 6 5 4 3 2 1

Library of Congress Cataloging-in-Publication Data
Library of Congress Control Number: 2006014333

ISBN-13: 978-1-56477-677-8
ISBN-10: 1-56477-677-8

Contents

Introduction

After two books, I'm still stacking, cutting, and sewing fabrics together to make even more fun quilts with my Stack the Deck method. Don't get me wrong: I still and will always enjoy making the "canned quilts"—that is, the ones for which carefully chosen fabrics, precision cutting, and perfect seam allowances are a must. I love and design many of these quilts for my business, Saginaw Street Quilt Company. However, the design possibilities presented by the Stack the Deck method are so liberating and so different, and always yield unusual and surprising blocks. In addition to the creative freedom, I get to use lots and lots of different fabrics. There are no duplications; every quilt is an original. Quilts may reflect my mood for the day with quiet and straight cuts or with wild and whacky ones. Of course, the style and colors of the fabric play a role as well.

I invite you to gather up some fabric and enjoy the freedom of straight, curvy, or funky-cut angles. You'll find this method useful for many projects, from making pieced fabric for handbags, jackets, and borders, to the most fun of all—making quilts!

A sewing machine in good working order, high-quality supplies and tools, accuracy in stitching, and a whole lot of passion are the ingredients in my recipe for a good quilting experience. The following is a rundown of the basic tools and techniques you'll need to make any of the quilts in this book. Refer back to this section as needed when you're making your quilt project.

TOOLS AND SUPPLIES

These tools will make your Crazy-quilt experience both fun and easy.

Rotary cutter. Choose a medium to large rotary cutter. Start with a sharp, new blade that will allow you to cut through several layers of fabric at a time.

Cutting mat. A mat that measures 18" x 24" should be sufficient for cutting blocks and borders. You might want to use one side for cutting curves and the other side for straight cuts.

Acrylic rulers. A 6" x 24" ruler is great for cutting fabric into strips. A square ruler is essential for cutting squares and trimming up pieced blocks. A 12½" square is best, but depending on your project, a 6" or smaller square ruler may be adequate.

Mounting tape. This double-sticky tape with foam backing comes on a roll and can be purchased at most hardware stores. I use this tape as a guide when sewing curved pieces.

Sewing thread. Use good-quality, 100%-cotton thread for piecing. Match the thread to the general value of the fabrics. In most cases, you can use neutral colors: light, medium, and dark values of tan and gray.

Quilting thread. Choosing your quilting thread is usually one of the last decisions to be made, but it is one of my favorite steps! I use a variety of thread, ranging from 100% cotton to silky rayons and metallics. Have fun choosing your thread and always buy the best you can afford; it will pay off in the end.

Seam ripper. Keep a seam ripper handy for easy stitch removal.

Sewing machine. Be sure your sewing machine is in good working order and sews a reliable and balanced straight stitch. If you plan to machine quilt, you will need a walking foot and possibly a darning foot, depending on the style of quilting you choose.

Basting spray (optional). Spray basting is a time-saver when layering the quilt sandwich for machine quilting. I don't recommend it for hand quilting.

FUSIBLE-WEB APPLIQUÉ

Several projects in this book include designs created with fusible-web appliqué. Paper-backed fusible web is sold in both heavyweight and lightweight varieties. For this book, I used the lightweight fusible web and added a machine buttonhole stitch, a straight stitch, a satin stitch, or a zigzag stitch over the raw edges of the appliqué shape. For appliqués that won't be stitched, I recommend that you use a heavier-weight fusible web. Since the fusible web is applied to the wrong side of the fabric, patterns for fusible-web appliqué are given in mirror image.

1. Trace each part of the selected appliqué design onto the paper side of the fusible web. Cut roughly around the traced designs on the fusible web. Don't cut on the traced lines at this point.

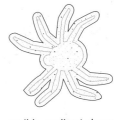

Fusible appliqué shape

2. Position each cut fusible shape, web side down, on the wrong side of the selected fabrics and press, following the manufacturer's directions for the fusible web. Cut out each shape on the drawn lines. Remove the paper backing.

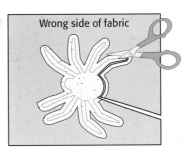

Wrong side of fabric

3. Arrange the shapes in the desired position on the right side of the background fabric. Use an iron to fuse the shapes in place according to the manufacturer's directions.

4. Sew around the edges of each appliqué shape using your desired stitch.

ASSEMBLING THE QUILT TOP

Once your blocks are made, arrange them by following the instructions and diagrams provided with the project. Play with the blocks—twisting, turning, and substituting them—until you're satisfied with the arrangement. I try to separate identical prints so that they don't end up next to each other in the finished quilt. With some projects, you'll have extra blocks to choose from. When you're happy with the arrangement, you can use any extra blocks to stitch up a coordinating pillow or incorporate into a label and stitch it to the back of your quilt.

Join the blocks in horizontal, vertical, or diagonal rows as directed, matching the seams between the blocks. Press the seams in the opposite direction from row to row so that opposing seams butt against each other, or follow the pressing arrows in the quilt diagrams.

For quilts with sashing strips and cornerstones, arrange the blocks, strips, and cornerstones as shown for the specific project. Sew the blocks and horizontal sashing strips into rows and press seams toward the sashing strips. Sew the cornerstones and vertical sashing strips into rows and press the seams toward the sashing strips. Sew the rows together to complete the quilt center.

ABOUT MATERIALS AND CUTTING

All yardages are based on 42"-wide fabrics, with 40" of usable width after preshrinking. When following the cutting instructions, cut all strips across the fabric width from selvage to selvage (cross grain).

ADDING BORDERS

1. Refer to the cutting directions for each quilt and cut the required number of strips for the border.

2. Remove the selvages and sew the border strips together with straight seams to make one continuous strip. Press the seams to one side.

3. Measure the length (top to bottom) of the quilt top through the center. Cut two border strips to that measurement. Mark the center of the quilt edges and the border strips.

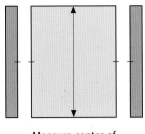

Measure center of
quilt, top to bottom.
Mark centers.

4. Pin the borders to opposite sides of the quilt, matching the center marks and ends and adding more pins as needed to ease in any fullness. Sew the borders in place with a ¼" seam. Press the seams toward the border.

5. Measure the width (side to side) of the quilt top through the center, including the borders just added. Cut two border strips to that measurement. Mark the centers, and pin and sew the borders to the top and bottom as described for the side borders. Press the seams toward the border.

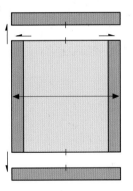

Measure center of quilt,
side to side, including borders.
Mark centers.

FINISHING THE QUILT

The following information will help you bring your quilting project to a successful conclusion.

LAYERING

The backing and batting should be at least 2" to 3" larger than the quilt top all around.

1. Prepare the backing as instructed for each project, piecing it as necessary.

BACKING SEAMS

When piecing your backing, press the seams to one side for a stronger seam. If you will be hand quilting, however, press them open to reduce bulk.

2. Lay out the backing, wrong side up, on a large table (or on top of a large sheet if spray basting; see page 8) and secure it with masking tape. Be careful not to stretch the backing too tightly, but just enough to keep it nice and smooth. If you don't have a large table, tack the backing to the floor by inserting T-pins into the carpet.

3. Center the batting on top of the backing. Smooth out any wrinkles.

4. Center the pieced top, right side up, on the batting. Make sure that the quilt top is "square" with the backing.

5. Baste the layers together, using one of the three techniques that follow. (My personal favorite is spray basting.)

Hand Basting

I recommend that you baste by hand if you will be hand quilting.

1. Thread a large needle with a long length of thread. Beginning in the center of the quilt, sew on the diagonal to each corner with large stitches.

2. Baste in a grid, stitching horizontal and vertical rows across the quilt top. Space the rows approximately 6" apart. Finish by stitching all around the perimeter of the quilt.

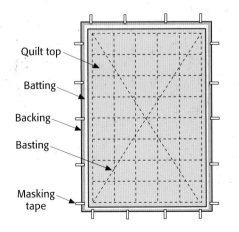

Quilt top
Batting
Backing
Basting
Masking
tape

Pin Basting

Pin baste if you plan to machine quilt. Pin basting is done most easily if you have a large table for laying out the quilt. Place 1" rustproof safety pins every 5" to 6" across the quilt top, beginning in the center and working your way to the outer edges. Place the pins where they won't interfere with your planned quilting stitches.

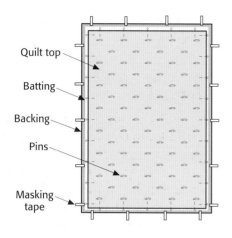

Quilt top
Batting
Backing
Pins
Masking tape

Spray Basting

Basting spray is a relatively new product that works extremely well with cotton and cotton-blend battings. Here are a few things to keep in mind for successful spray basting:

- Make sure you work in a well-ventilated area.
- Place a large sheet under your quilt to catch any overspray.
- Make doubly sure the backing is securely anchored and wrinkle-free!

To spray baste, follow these steps.

1. Arrange the backing, batting, and quilt top on a large sheet. Secure with tape or T-pins.

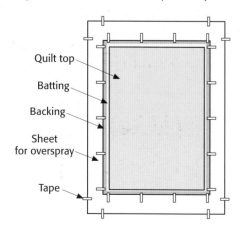

Quilt top
Batting
Backing
Sheet for overspray
Tape

2. Fold the quilt top down, horizontally, about a quarter of the way down; fold down again so that half the quilt top is folded on itself in quarters and the batting is exposed.

3. Repeat with the batting, folding it in quarters to expose the upper half of the backing.

4. Lightly spray the back of the exposed quarter of batting. Gently replace the batting on the backing. Slide the can of basting spray over the top of the sprayed batting to smooth out any wrinkles. Lightly spray the back of the remaining quarter of exposed batting and then carefully replace it on the backing, smoothing out any wrinkles.

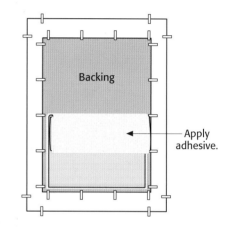

Backing

Apply adhesive.

5. Lightly spray a quarter of the front of the exposed batting (not the quilt top!) and replace a quarter of the folded quilt top onto the batting. Smooth out any wrinkles. Repeat for the remaining quarter of the quilt top.

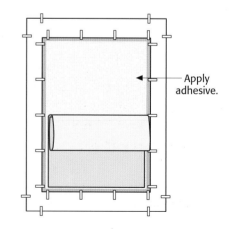

Apply adhesive.

6. When you've finished with half of the quilt, repeat steps 2–5 for the opposite half of the quilt, always working in quarters. When you've finished, remove the tape or T-pins and turn the basted quilt over. Carefully smooth out any wrinkles.

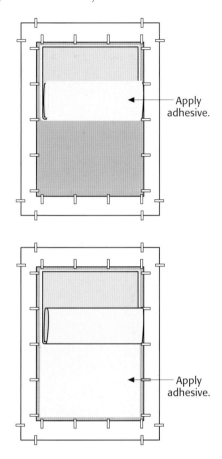

Apply adhesive.

Apply adhesive.

BINDING

Binding finishes the edges of your quilt. I prefer a double-fold, straight-grain binding, often referred to as a French-fold binding. I often choose one of the prints I've used in the quilt top for the binding, but sometimes I introduce a new fabric. Since I frequently use busy prints in my quilts, I might choose a coordinating print that reads as a solid from a distance.

1. Trim the batting and backing even with the quilt top.

2. Refer to the cutting list for each individual project and cut the required number of strips for binding.

3. Remove the selvages and place the strips right sides together as shown. Sew the strips together with diagonal seams to make one long binding strip. Trim the excess fabric, leaving a 1/4" seam allowance, and press the seams open to reduce bulk.

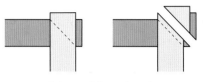

Joining straight-grain strips

4. Fold the strip in half lengthwise, wrong sides together, and press.

5. Beginning about 18" from a corner, place the binding right sides together with the quilt top. Align the raw edges. Leave a 10" tail and use a 1/4" seam allowance and a walking foot to sew the binding to the front of your quilt. Stop sewing 1/4" from the first corner and carefully backstitch two or three stitches. Clip the thread and remove the quilt from the machine.

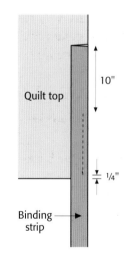

Quilt top

10"

1/4"

Binding strip

6. Rotate the quilt 90° so that you can work on the next side. Fold the binding up, creating a 45° angle, and then back down, even with the second side of the quilt. A little pleat will form at the corner.

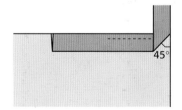

45°

7. Resume stitching at the folded edge of the binding as shown. Continue stitching the binding to the quilt, turning the corners as described, until you are approximately 10" from the point at which you started sewing the binding. Remove the quilt from the sewing machine.

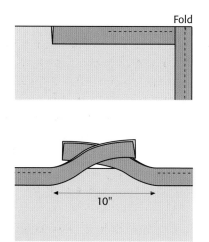

8. Fold back the beginning and ending tails of the binding strips so that they meet in the center of the unsewn portion of the quilt edge. Finger-press the folded edges.

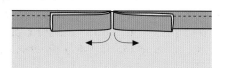

9. Unfold both ends of the binding and match the center points of the two finger-pressed folds, forming an X as shown. Pin and sew the two ends together on the diagonal of the fold lines. Trim the excess binding ¼" from the seam. Finger-press the

new seam allowance open and refold the binding. Finish sewing the binding to the quilt.

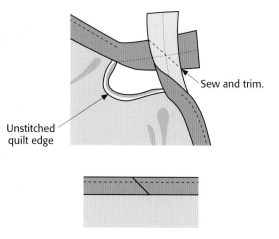

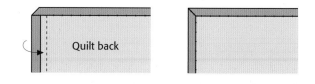

10. Fold the binding over the edge of the quilt top to the back of the quilt, making sure to cover the machine stitching. Hand sew the binding in place, mitering the corners as you go.

LABELING YOUR QUILT

Finish your quilt by adding a label to the back. The label should, at a minimum, include your name and date. Add other information as desired: the name of the quilt, your hometown, the recipient's name, the occasion, and so on. Use a permanent fabric marker to write the information on a piece of fabric and then hand sew it to the back of your quilt. You'll find it easier to write on the fabric if you press a piece of freezer paper to the wrong side first. Remove the freezer paper before sewing the label to the quilt.

Making the Blocks, Stack the Deck Style

Almost all the quilts in this book lend themselves well to beginning and intermediate quiltmakers; however, it's always a good idea to feel confident in the stacking, cutting, shuffling, and sewing process before attacking a large project. I suggest reading this chapter in full before beginning any of the projects.

CHOOSING FABRIC

Each project lists the number of blocks you'll need to make. The fun (and sometimes challenging) part of the process is selecting all the different fabrics. I like to choose a fabric theme, such as batiks, bright juvenile prints, or floral prints. Then I apply my 10-Foot Rule (see the next section) to help narrow down my choices and make sure there's sufficient visual contrast in the fabrics I've selected. I like to browse through my stash and challenge myself to use up leftovers.

As long as you cut the fabrics according to the requirements, you usually can use as many different fabrics within one color group as you like. For example, if the fabric requirements call for 10 turquoise squares, you can use 10 entirely different prints as long as they are in the turquoise range. Keep in mind that the quilts in the photographs often use a larger variety of fabrics than the minimum listed, giving you the opportunity to use many of the fabrics you already own.

THE 10-FOOT RULE

If you are purchasing new fabric, stack the bolts of fabric, one on top of another, on the counter or stand them side by side. If you are working from your stash, fold and stack the fabrics on your worktable and fan them out. Then back up approximately 10 feet and take a look. Do the fabrics contrast well with one another? Does one fabric jump out from the rest? If so, it may need a "companion." For example, if you have just one red fabric in the mix and your eye goes right to it every time you look at the stack, try adding another red (or two) to the mix for a better balance.

On the other hand, if you have three fabrics from the same color group, use the 10-Foot Rule to determine if they appear to blend together too much, resembling a single piece of fabric. Instead of having three medium blues that all muddle together, swap one out for a brighter blue, a blue that has another color in the print, or something to liven up the group. If you have three grass greens that don't seem too exciting, swap in some lime, chartreuse, or sage for a peppier mix.

One of my favorite tools for evaluating fabric is a simple door peephole, available at any home-improvement center. Looking through a door peephole distances you from your fabric choices and helps you determine if you have a "jumper" (a fabric that jumps out at you) or too many fabrics that blend together. Also now available at most quilt stores is a fabric-reducing tool, which looks a lot like a magnifying glass. It is much larger than the door peephole, making the viewing process even easier.

STACKING THE DECK

Once you've selected a quilt to make, refer to the specific fabric requirements for that project. The individual project directions will tell you how many decks of fabric you need, how many fabrics in a deck, and what size squares or rectangles to start with. Cut the required number of pieces and then stack them right side up for rotary cutting. Alternate contrasting colors and/or values as directed in the specific quilt instructions. Make sure you haven't duplicated the same fabric in any one deck unless directed to do so. Keep in mind also that in most decks, the top fabric will eventually be rotated to the bottom, so it's a good idea to make sure the top and bottom fabrics contrast as well. Many quilts in this book have a large variety and number of fabrics—why use four fabrics when you can use 40?—and it's likely some of the same fabrics will eventually end up side by side somewhere in the quilt, but you'll want to keep that occurrence to a minimum.

SLICING THE DECK

Now that your decks are all neatly stacked and ready to go, you have two options for cutting them into segments: you can make a cutting template out of paper or slice the deck freehand. Each project includes a "Block Cutting, Shuffling, and Sewing Guide." The guide features a diagram in which the cutting order is listed numerically in red and the sewing order is listed numerically in blue. You'll refer to these markings often as you work on the blocks.

MAKING A PAPER TEMPLATE

Your first option for slicing the deck is to make full-size paper templates to place over the fabric decks so that you can establish cutting guidelines. To do this, cut a piece of plain white paper, freezer paper, or wrapping paper (unprinted side up) the same size as the cut fabric (such as squares and rectangles). Then transfer the cutting lines as closely as possible to those on the diagram in the "Block Cutting, Shuffling, and Sewing Guide" that appears with the project. Make as many copies as there are fabric decks in the project. Don't worry if your version isn't *exactly* the same as the diagram. I usually vary mine on purpose!

VARY THE ANGLES

Varying the angles on your template from one deck to another will give you more variety and interest in your finished quilt. Most quilts in this book were made using a specific template; however, with each new deck, I changed the lines and angles slightly.

Whole-Segment Template

Whole-segment templates may have as many as eight segments and as few as two. With this style of template, often you sew the segments together in the same order in which you cut them.

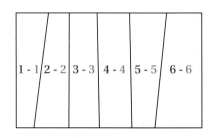

Whole segment template.
The red number is the cutting order.
The blue number is the sewing order.

Chipped Template

With this style of template, you split the deck into two or more sections, then you "chip" or slice each set into two or more sections. You shuffle the deck, piece each set of "chips" together separately, and then sew the segments together to complete the block. Often you sew the segments in reverse order from the order in which you cut them; that is, you join the last two segments you cut first, then you sew the segment you cut before the last two segments to the combined unit, and so on.

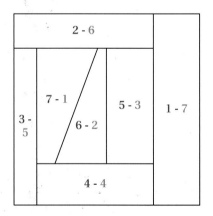

Chipped template.
The red number is the cutting order.
The blue number is the sewing order.

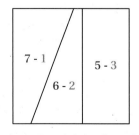

Inside section of chipped template.
Sew the center pieces together to make one section before sewing to the remaining pieces.

CUTTING WITH A PAPER TEMPLATE

1. Place the paper template on top of your fabric deck. Pin the pattern to the deck, pinning through each numbered segment to secure it.

EASY PINNING

Since you'll be placing your acrylic ruler over the pins for cutting, flat-head flower pins work very well with paper templates.

2. Use your rotary cutter and ruler to slice through the paper template on every solid line, cutting through all layers of fabric.

3. Remove the pins and paper template. Reassemble the template (like a jigsaw puzzle) to the side of the cut blocks for reference. Now you're ready to "shuffle the deck" as described in "Shuffling Basics" on page 14.

CUTTING CURVES

When cutting curves, with or without a template, gently slide your ruler along the edge of the curve as you cut.

FREE-FORM CUTTING

If you don't want to make a paper template for each stack of fabric squares, you can cut the deck free-form. Refer to the block diagram that appears in the "Block Cutting, Shuffling, and Sewing Guide" for the project, and use a chalk marker to draw the cutting lines directly onto the fabric deck. This is easy to do, and you can brush the lines away if you don't like the outcome and redraw until you do. Unless noted otherwise in the specific project instructions, you can vary the lines from one deck to the next. This gives each deck its own individual style.

Once you're satisfied with the lines, lay your rotary ruler on top of the stacked fabrics and cut the deck apart on the chalk lines, making the first cut as indicated in the block diagram. Keeping the deck together, shift the ruler to make the next cut. Continue cutting the pieces apart, referring to the block drawing as you go.

Now you're ready to "shuffle the deck" as described in the next section.

NUMBER OF CUTS AND BLOCK SIZE

The more segments that appear in the template, the more cuts and seams you'll need to make. As a result, the finished blocks will be smaller than those with fewer cuts and seams.

SHUFFLING BASICS

There are two different shuffling methods used for the projects in this book: the traditional shuffle and the controlled shuffle. The instructions for each individual quilt will tell you which method to use.

TRADITIONAL SHUFFLING

Traditional shuffling is always the same process, regardless of how many segments there are in your particular block. Whether you have two segments or eight segments, you shuffle each segment stack just once. For the projects in this book, the segment stack number is the same as the sewing order number, or blue number.

1. Remove the top layer from the segment 1 stack and place it on the bottom of that stack.

2. Remove two layers of fabric from the segment 2 stack and place them on the bottom of that stack.

3. Remove three layers of fabric from the segment 3 stack and place them on the bottom of that stack. Continue shuffling each stack, removing the same number of fabrics from the top as the number of the segment you are shuffling, until all blocks have been shuffled. If the number of fabric layers is equal to the number of cut segments, you don't need to shuffle the last segment stack. For instance, if you have a deck of six squares and are cutting a six-segment block, you need only shuffle the first five segments because the last set is already in place.

CONTROLLED SHUFFLING

You'll use controlled shuffling when, rather than all segments, only specific segments are shuffled a certain number of times (see "Safari" on page 26). Shuffling only certain pieces gives the block its unique appearance. For example, "S-1" means remove *one* layer and place it at the bottom of the segment stack; "S-2" means remove *two* layers, and so on.

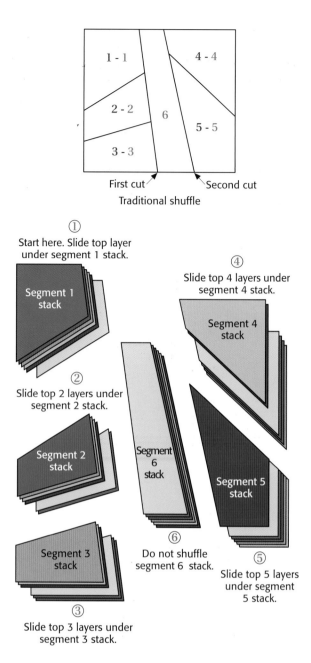

Traditional shuffle

① Start here. Slide top layer under segment 1 stack.

Segment 1 stack

② Slide top 2 layers under segment 2 stack.

Segment 2 stack

③ Slide top 3 layers under segment 3 stack.

Segment 3 stack

④ Slide top 4 layers under segment 4 stack.

Segment 4 stack

⑤ Slide top 5 layers under segment 5 stack.

Segment 5 stack

⑥ Do not shuffle segment 6 stack.

Segment 6 stack

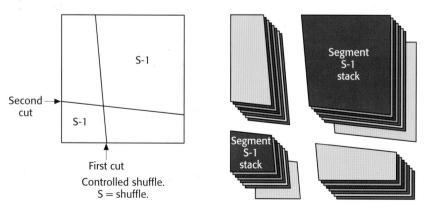

Controlled shuffle.
S = shuffle.

Segment S-1 stack

Shuffle the S-1 segments by sliding the top layer under the stack. The remaining pieces stay in place.

PREPARING A PAPER LAYOUT

This is a *very important* step! Please do not skip it. Regardless of the method you use, once you've completed the shuffling process, reassemble the block and pin each stack of segments to a piece of paper through all layers. Be sure to keep the segment stacks in the exact order and layout in which you shuffled them. Once the segments are secure, use a pencil and trace along the cutting lines onto the paper. The pins will help keep the segments in order, and the lines will create a template reference.

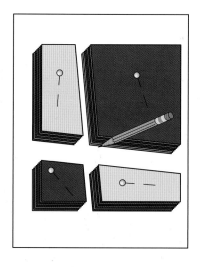

SEWING THE BLOCKS

To determine where to begin sewing, refer to the blue numbers in the block diagram in the "Block Cutting, Shuffling, and Sewing Guide" for the project you're making. These numbers indicate the sewing order. (You'll notice that the sewing order is often the exact opposite order of how you cut the segments. For instance, the last piece sliced into two segments will be numbered 1 and 2 in blue in the block diagram, indicating that these will be the first two segments to sew, and so on.) Once you've determined the sewing order, use a pencil to note the number on the paper beneath the appropriate segment.

It is important that you keep the segment stacks in their shuffled order while sewing; otherwise you'll end up duplicating a fabric within the same block. For instance, after chain piecing (see right) all layers of the segment 1 stack and the segment 2 stack together, always return the units to their original order. It's easy to reverse the order while ironing and/or clipping the segments apart, *so I strongly recommend that you place a safety pin in the top layer of the segment 1 stack.* That way, when you begin sewing again, you'll auto-matically know the combined segments are in the right sequence if the safety pin is on top of the stack. If the safety pin is *not* on top of the stack, you'll know you probably reversed the order and you will need to correct it before you continue. Keep the safety pin in place until you've sewn all the blocks in the deck.

PIECING WHOLE BLOCKS

1. Unpin the segment 1 and 2 stacks and peel off the top pieces from each stack. Flip piece 2 onto piece 1 with right sides facing, and stitch the pieces together.

2. Pick up the next layer from the segment 1 and 2 stacks and sew them together in the same manner. You can chain piece the units together as shown, continuing until you've stitched all the segment 1 and segment 2 pieces together in pairs.

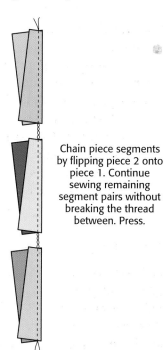

Chain piece segments by flipping piece 2 onto piece 1. Continue sewing remaining segment pairs without breaking the thread between. Press.

3. Press the 1-2 units open with the seam allowance to either side. Then clip the units apart and restack them in their original order.

4. Peel the top segment from stack 3 and sew, right sides together, with the 1-2 units from step 3. Don't

be surprised if the new edges of additional segments don't line up evenly with the combined units; they more than likely will not. Just match them together as best as you can, making sure your seam is at least ¼" from all raw edges.

Continue adding segments (in numerical order) to each combined unit.

5. Press the units open, clip them apart, and stack them in their original order. Continue adding segments in numerical order until you've added all the segments.

PIECING MULTISIDED CHIPPED BLOCKS

The method for sewing blocks with two or more chipped sections is exactly the same as sewing whole blocks, with the exception that you piece each chipped section separately and then piece together the individual sections.

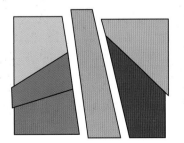

TRIMMING

Due to the seam allowances, the pieced segments will shrink up and tend to be smaller than the segment they are added to. To remedy this, refer to your paper layout and trim the excess fabric as you go to even the edges for the next piece. Return to the paper layout and continue chain piecing, making sure to maintain the original order.

When the blocks are complete, place a square rotary ruler on top of each finished block and trim to the size specified in the project instructions.

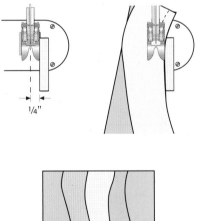

SEWING CURVES

Many quilts in this book have blocks that include slight curves. It is always a good idea to mark the center of the curve on both pieces and pin to keep the pieces aligned for sewing. To piece them with a minimum of pinning or clipping, place mounting tape (see page 5) on the bed of your sewing machine to use as a guide. Press a 1" to 2" strip of tape ¼" from the needle, extending it in front of the presser foot as shown. Gently align the curved edges of the fabric approximately 1" to 2" in front of the needle and up against the edge of the mounting tape as you sew. Since the blocks will be trimmed to size later, you don't need to fuss with matching the bottom edges!

¼"

Gently align raw edges against the tape as you sew. Align only a short section, and don't match the bottom edges.

Aurora Aura

Finished Quilt: 55¾" x 75"

Finished Block A: 5¼" x 7"

Finished Block B: 5¼ x 6½"

I've always been intrigued by Chinese Coin quilts with their vertical rows made from strips of fabric sewn together in horizontal stacks. I decided to design "Aurora Aura" with this style in mind, using a range of my favorite colors: blue, purple, and green. Making this quilt is really quite simple because there are no seams to match, and the finished size of the blocks is determined by your own personal measurement!

FABRIC TIPS

The fabrics in this quilt are reminiscent of my view of the aurora borealis when I lived on Kodiak Island, Alaska. I began by choosing six medium-value greens that seemed to swirl together nicely for the aurora borealis. Next, I chose colors for the sky, which often reflect into the sea as different blues, greens, and turquoises.

MATERIALS

All yardages are based on 42"-wide fabric.

1¼ yards of bluish purple fabric for outer border

½ yard *each* of 3 assorted turquoise fabrics for blocks

½ yard *each* of 3 assorted greenish blue fabrics for blocks

½ yard *each* of 3 assorted purple fabrics for blocks

⅓ yard of reddish purple fabric for inner border

¼ yard *each* of 6 assorted medium green fabrics for sashing

⅝ yard of fabric for binding

3⅓ yards of fabric for backing

60" x 80" piece of batting

CUTTING

Cut all strips across the fabric width (cross grain). Measurements for sashing, borders, and binding include the traditional ¼" seam allowances.

From *each* turquoise, greenish blue, and purple fabric, cut:

2 strips, 6" x 42" (18 total); crosscut into
    5 rectangles, 6" x 10" (45 total)

From *each* medium green fabric, cut:

1 strip, 2½" x 42"; crosscut into:
    1 piece, 2½" x 11"
    1 piece, 2½" x 9"
    1 piece, 2½" x 7"
    1 piece, 2½" x 5"
    1 piece, 2½" x 3"
    1 piece, 2½" x 2"

1 strip, 3½" x 42"; crosscut into:
    1 piece, 3½" x 11"
    1 piece, 3½" x 9"
    1 piece, 3½" x 7"
    1 piece, 3½" x 5"
    1 piece, 3½" x 3"
    1 piece, 3½" x 2"

From the reddish purple fabric, cut:

6 strips, 1½" x 42"

From the bluish purple fabric, cut:

6 strips, 6½" x 42"

From the binding fabric, cut:

7 strips, 2½" x 42"

Block Cutting, Shuffling, and Sewing Guide

Cut Size: 6" x 10"

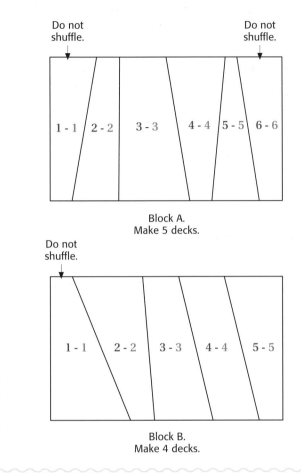

Block A.
Make 5 decks.

Block B.
Make 4 decks.

Refer to "Making the Blocks, Stack the Deck Style" on page 11 for guidance as needed. These blocks are shuffled using the traditional shuffling technique described on page 14. If you are using a cutting template, use the whole-segment template technique described on page 12.

1. Arrange the 6" x 10" assorted turquoise, greenish blue, and purple rectangles into nine decks of five rectangles each, right sides up, alternating the colors. Each deck should contain a different mix of fabrics. Secure each deck with a pin through all the layers.

2. Divide the decks into two sets: five for block A and four for block B. Working with one deck at a time, cut and shuffle the pieces as shown in the appropriate diagram at left. (Notice that the first piece of each A and B deck remains unshuffled.) Vary the width and angle of the cuts from deck to deck so that all decks are cut a little differently from one another. As you go, secure each deck to a piece of paper by pinning through all the layers.

   After shuffling, you'll notice that the first and last segment of block A are the same fabric. This is fine; however, I often shuffle a few more segments under just to vary the mix. This works well as long as duplicate fabrics never touch.

MAKING THE BLOCKS

1. Referring to "Sewing the Blocks" on page 15 and the diagrams above and at right, sew the shuffled segments for each block together. Press the seams to one side. Make 25 A blocks and 20 B blocks (45 total).

2. Trim the A blocks to 5³⁄₄" x 7". Trim the B blocks to 5³⁄₄" x 7¹⁄₂". These lengths are approximate, so it's OK if you're unable to get the full length.

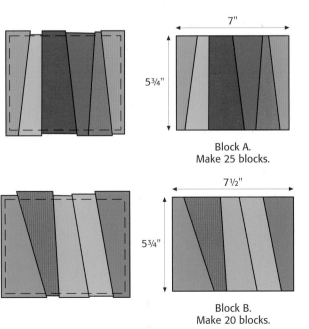

Block A.
Make 25 blocks.

Block B.
Make 20 blocks.

MAKING THE PIECED SASHING

1. With right sides up, sort and stack the 2½"-wide and 3½"-wide sashing strips by size.

2. Randomly mix the fabrics and sew the 2½"-wide strips together end to end to make one strip approximately 210" long; press. Repeat with the 3½"-wide strips.

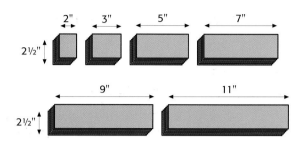

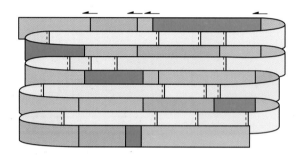

ASSEMBLING THE QUILT TOP

Refer to "Assembling the Quilt Top" on page 6 for guidance as needed.

1. Arrange the blocks into five vertical rows of nine blocks each, alternating the A and B blocks as shown. Arrange the blocks so that the seams run horizontally. Move, turn, and mix the A blocks with the B blocks until you are satisfied with your arrangement. Make sure identical prints aren't touching in the finished layout. View your arrangement through a door peephole (see "The 10-Foot Rule" on page 11) to check the color and block balance.

2. Pin and sew the blocks into vertical rows; press. Rows should measure approximately 61" in length. Measure each row and note the length of the shortest row. Trim the remaining rows to this length.

Make 5.

3. Measure and cut each 2½"-wide and 3½"-wide pieced sashing strip into three lengths, each equal to the length you determined in step 2.

4. Select two rows from step 2 and trim a 3½"-wide strip from one long side by sliding the row over your cutting mat and using a rotary ruler and cutter to measure and cut the strip. This will create four skinny rows: two 3½" wide and two 2¼" wide.

5. Arrange the remaining rows from step 2, the trimmed rows from step 4, and the trimmed sashing strips from step 3 as desired. The assembly diagram below shows the arrangement I used for my "Aurora Aura" quilt.

6. Pin and sew the rows and/or sashing strips together in six pairs. Pin and sew the last row to the sixth pair; press.

7. Pin and sew the first three units from step 6 together. Repeat with the second three units; press.

8. Pin and sew the two units from step 7 together; press.

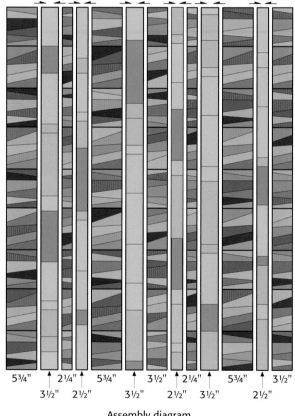

Assembly diagram

ADDING THE BORDERS

1. Refer to "Adding Borders" on page 6. Sew the 1½"-wide reddish purple strips together end to end to make one long inner-border strip.

2. Measure the length of the quilt top through the center and cut two inner-border strips to this measurement. Pin and sew the borders to the sides of the quilt. Press the seams toward the border strips. Measure the width of the quilt top through the center, including the borders just added, and cut two inner-border strips to this measurement. Pin and sew the borders to the top and bottom of the quilt; press.

3. Repeat steps 1 and 2 with the 6½"-wide bluish purple strips to make and attach the outer border.

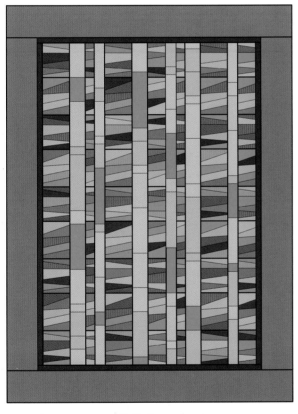

Quilt diagram

FINISHING

Refer to "Finishing the Quilt" on page 7 as needed.

1. Divide the backing fabric crosswise into two equal panels, each approximately 60" long. Remove the selvages and sew the pieces together along the long edges to make a backing piece approximately 60" x 80"; press.

2. Layer the quilt top with the batting and backing, keeping the backing seam parallel to the short edges of the quilt top. Baste the layers together using your favorite method.

3. Hand or machine quilt as desired.

4. Trim the backing and batting even with the edges of the quilt top and use the 2½"-wide strips to bind the quilt.

QUILTING SUGGESTIONS

I quilted in the ditch to anchor each row and to anchor the borders as well. I machine quilted with variegated purple, pink, and blue thread, using a whimsical freestyle stitch through the width of the blocks and the sashing, and finished with light overall stipple quilting in the borders.

Four Patch Fusion

Finished Quilt: 53" x 72"

Finished Block: 5½" x 5½"

Working with black-and-white prints often suggests a touch of whimsy to me and this quilt was no exception!

FABRIC TIPS

Look for a variety of small- to medium-scale white prints with black backgrounds as well as black prints with white backgrounds. To accent the black and white, choose bright, clear colors for the sashing.

MATERIALS

All yardages are based on 42"-wide fabric.

1 1/8 yards of turquoise print for outer border

1/3 yard of black fabric for inner border

1/4 yard *each* of 8 assorted black-with-white-background prints for blocks and cornerstones

1/4 yard *each* of 8 assorted white-with-black-background prints for blocks and cornerstones

1/4 yard *each* of 9 prints in assorted colors (for example, red, gold, blue, and purple) for sashing

5/8 yard of fabric for binding

3 1/4 yards of fabric for backing

58" x 78" piece of batting

CUTTING

Cut all strips across the fabric width (cross grain).

From the assorted black-with-white-background prints, cut a *total* of:

27 squares, 6 1/2" x 6 1/2"

From the assorted white-with-black-background prints, cut a *total* of:

27 squares, 6 1/2" x 6 1/2"

From the remaining assortment of black-with-white-background *and* white-with-black-background prints, cut a *total* of:

70 squares, 1 1/2" x 1 1/2"

From the prints in assorted colors, cut a *total* of:

123 strips, 1 1/2" x 6"

From the black fabric, cut:

6 strips, 1 1/2" x 42"

From the turquoise print, cut:

6 strips, 5 3/4" x 42"

From the binding fabric, cut:

7 strips, 2 1/2" x 42"

Block Cutting, Shuffling, and Sewing Guide

Cut Size: 6½" x 6½"

```
            ┌──────┬──────┐
            │      │      │
            │ S-1  │ S-2  │
            │      │      │
Second cut ─┼──────┼──────┤
  (3¼")     │      │      │
            │ S-4  │ S-3  │
            │      │      │
            └──────┴──────┘
                   ↑
           First cut (3¼")
```

Make 9 decks.
S = shuffle.

Refer to "Making the Blocks, Stack the Deck Style" on page 11 for guidance as needed. These blocks are shuffled using the traditional shuffling technique described on page 14. If you are using a cutting template, use the chipped template technique described on page 12.

1. Arrange the 6½" assorted black and white squares into nine decks of six squares each, right sides up, alternating the white and black prints. Each deck should contain a different mix of fabrics. Secure each deck with a pin through all the layers.

2. Working with one deck at a time, cut and shuffle the pieces as shown in the diagram above. As you go, secure each deck to a piece of paper by pinning through all the layers.

MAKING THE BLOCKS

Referring to "Sewing the Blocks" on page 15 and the diagram below, sew the shuffled segments for each block together to make a Four Patch block. Sew the segments together in pairs; press. Sew the pairs together; press. The blocks should measure 6" x 6". Make 54.

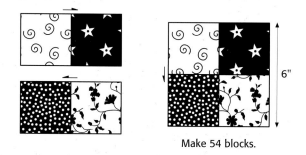

Make 54 blocks.

ASSEMBLING THE QUILT TOP

Refer to "Assembling the Quilt Top" on page 6 for guidance as needed.

1. Arrange the blocks into six vertical rows of nine blocks each as shown in the assembly diagram on page 25, leaving space between the blocks for the sashing strips. Rotate the blocks as shown so that both the white squares and the black squares form secondary Four Patch blocks and so that identical prints aren't side by side. Once you are satisfied with the layout, add the 1½" x 6" assorted sashing strips and 1½"-square black and white cornerstones. View your arrangement through a door peephole (see "The 10-Foot Rule" on page 11) to check the color and block balance.

2. Sew the blocks and horizontal sashing strips together into vertical rows. Press the seams toward the sashing strips. Make six rows, replacing them in the layout as you go.

3. Sew the vertical sashing strips and cornerstones together into vertical rows. Press the seams toward the cornerstones. Make seven rows, replacing them in the layout as you go.

4. Sew the sashing/cornerstone rows from step 3 to the block/sashing rows from step 2. Press the seams toward the sashing/cornerstone rows. Sew the remaining sashing/cornerstone row to the last pair; press.

5. Pin and sew the units from step 4 together in three sets of two units each; press.

6. Pin and sew the units from step 5 together; press.

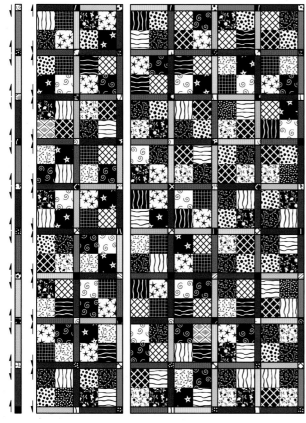

Assembly diagram

Quilt plan

ADDING THE BORDERS

1. Refer to "Adding Borders" on page 6. Sew the 1½"-wide black strips together end to end to make one long inner-border strip.

2. Measure the length of the quilt top through the center and cut two inner-border strips to this measurement. Pin and sew the borders to the sides of the quilt. Press the seams toward the border strips. Measure the width of the quilt top through the center, including the borders just added, and cut two inner-border strips to this measurement. Pin and sew the borders to the top and bottom of the quilt; press.

3. Repeat steps 1 and 2 with the 5¾"-wide turquoise print strips to make and attach the outer border.

FINISHING

Refer to "Finishing the Quilt" on page 7 as needed.

1. Divide the backing fabric crosswise into two equal panels, each approximately 58" long. Remove the selvages and sew the pieces together along the long edges to make a backing piece approximately 58" x 80"; press.

2. Layer the quilt top with the batting and backing, keeping the backing seam parallel to the short edges of the quilt top. Baste the layers together using your favorite method.

3. Hand or machine quilt as desired.

4. Trim the backing and batting even with the edges of the quilt top and use the 2½"-wide strips to bind the quilt.

QUILTING SUGGESTIONS

I machine quilted in the ditch between the block and sashing rows. I also machine quilted diagonally through the blocks and finished with light overall stipple quilting for the borders.

Safari

Finished Quilt: 57½" x 79½"
Finished Block: 5½" x 5½"

The richness of jungle prints always has me stop to take a second and third look, and these exotic prints usually end up coming home with me. The prints in this quilt represent many of the colors found in jungle animals and, when coupled with the wild, uneven Four Patch blocks, create a quilt with a true safari look.

FABRIC TIPS

Search your local quilt stores for fun collections of jungle-style prints and choose a variety in light and dark values. Of course, any fabric family will work as long as you use contrasting light and dark prints.

MATERIALS

All yardages are based on 42"-wide fabric.

¼ yard *each* of 14 assorted light or medium (for example, gold, light brown, and medium green) prints for blocks

¼ yard *each* of 14 assorted dark (for example, black, dark brown, and dark green) prints for blocks

1¼ yards of burgundy fabric for outer border

½ yard of green fabric for inner border

⅔ yard of fabric for binding

4¾ yards of fabric for backing

62" x 84" piece of batting

CUTTING

Cut all strips across the fabric width (cross grain).

From *each* light or medium print, cut:

1 strip, 6½" x 42"; crosscut into 4 squares, 6½" x 6½" (56 total; you will use 48)

From *each* dark print, cut:

1 strip, 6½" x 42"; crosscut into 4 squares, 6½" x 6½" (56 total; you will use 48)

From the green fabric, cut:

6 strips, 2" x 42"

From the burgundy fabric, cut:

7 strips, 5½" x 42"

From the binding fabric, cut:

8 strips, 2½" x 42"

Block Cutting, Shuffling, and Sewing Guide

Cut Size: 6½" x 6½"

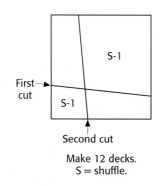

Make 12 decks.
S = shuffle.

Refer to "Making the Blocks, Stack the Deck Style" on page 11 for guidance as needed. These blocks are shuffled using the controlled shuffling technique described on page 14. If you are using a cutting template, use the chipped template technique described on page 12.

1. Arrange the 6½" assorted print squares into 12 decks of eight squares each, right sides up, alternating the light and medium fabrics with the dark fabrics. Each deck should contain a different mix of fabrics. Secure each deck with a pin through all the layers.

2. Working with one deck at a time, cut and shuffle the pieces as shown in the diagram above. As you go, secure each deck to a piece of paper by pinning through all the layers.

MAKING THE BLOCKS

Referring to "Sewing the Blocks" on page 15 and the diagrams at upper right, sew the shuffled segments for each block together to make a skewed Four Patch block. Sew the segments together to make two pairs as shown;

press. Sew the pairs together; press. Trim the blocks to 5½" x 5½". Make 96.

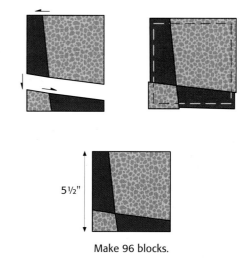

Make 96 blocks.

ASSEMBLING THE QUILT TOP

Refer to "Assembling the Quilt Top" on page 6 for guidance as needed.

1. Arrange the blocks into eight vertical rows of 12 blocks each, rotating the blocks and positioning them so that darks and lights are opposite one another as often as possible, as shown in the quilt photo on page 26. Make sure identical prints aren't touching in the finished layout. View your arrangement through a door peephole (see "The 10-Foot Rule" on page 11) to check the color and block balance.

2. Sew four blocks together, two blocks across by two blocks down, to make a jumbo-sized block, pressing as shown. Make 24.

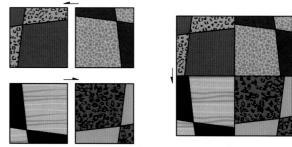

Make 24.

3. Pin and sew the jumbo-sized blocks into four vertical rows of six blocks each as shown in the assembly diagram on page 29; press.

4. Pin and sew the rows from step 3 together in pairs; press.

5. Pin and sew the pairs together; press, re-pressing any seams as needed to make construction easier.

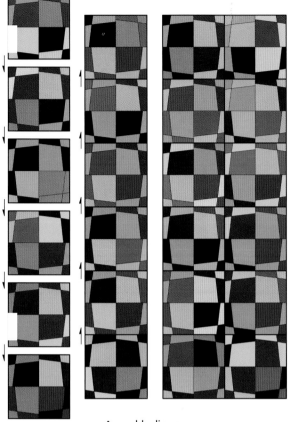

Assembly diagram

ADDING THE BORDERS

1. Refer to "Adding Borders" on page 6. Sew the 2"-wide green strips together end to end to make one long inner-border strip.

2. Measure the length of the quilt top through the center and cut two inner-border strips to this measurement. Pin and sew the borders to the sides of the quilt. Press the seams toward the border strips. Measure the width of the quilt top through the center, including the borders just added, and cut two inner-border strips to this measurement. Pin and sew the borders to the top and bottom of the quilt; press.

3. Repeat steps 1 and 2 with the 5½"-wide burgundy strips to make and attach the outer border.

FINISHING

Refer to "Finishing the Quilt" on page 7 as needed.

1. Divide the backing fabric crosswise into two equal panels, each approximately 85" long. Remove the selvages and sew the pieces together along the long edges to make a backing piece approximately 80" x 85"; press. Trim the backing to 2" to 3" larger than the quilt top all around.

2. Layer the quilt top with the batting and backing, keeping the backing seam parallel to the long edges of the quilt top. Baste the layers together using your favorite method.

3. Hand or machine quilt as desired.

4. Trim the backing and batting even with the edges of the quilt top and use the 2½"-wide strips to bind the quilt.

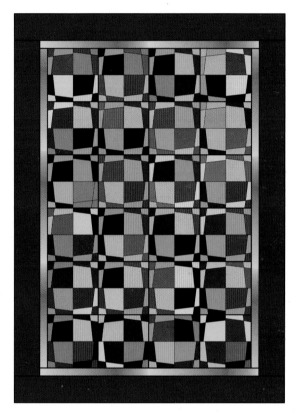

Quilt plan

QUILTING SUGGESTIONS

I stippled oval shapes throughout the blocks to look like rocks. I finished with traditional, overall stipple quilting in the border.

Wiggle in the Middle

Finished Quilt: 61½" x 76"

Finished Block: 4" x 6¼"

This quilt is made up of diagonally divided rectangles. Instead of a straight diagonal line cut from corner to corner, the blocks have a wiggle halfway through the cut. In order for four blocks to come together to form a diamond, half the blocks are cut from right to left and the remaining half are cut from left to right.

FABRIC TIP

For this quilt, I combined a variety of light pastel batiks with a variety of medium-value batiks.

MATERIALS

All yardages are based on 42"-wide fabric.

1⅓ yards of purple print for outer border

⅜ yard *each* of 8 assorted light (for example, pink, yellow, and tan) batiks for blocks

⅜ yard *each* of 8 assorted medium (for example, blue, green, and purple) batiks for blocks

⅓ yard of light green fabric for inner border

⅔ yard of fabric for binding

4⅝ yards of fabric for backing

66" x 82" piece of batting

CUTTING

Cut all strips across the fabric width (cross grain).

From *each* light batik, cut:

2 strips, 5" x 42"; crosscut into 8 rectangles, 5" x 7¾" (64 total; you will use 60)

From *each* medium batik, cut:

2 strips, 5" x 42"; crosscut into 8 rectangles, 5" x 7¾" (64 total; you will use 60)

From the light green fabric, cut:

6 strips, 1½" x 42"

From the purple print, cut:

7 strips, 6" x 42"

From the binding fabric, cut:

8 strips, 2½" x 42"

Block Cutting, Shuffling, and Sewing Guide

Cut Size: 5" x 7¾"

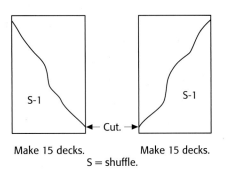

Make 15 decks.   Make 15 decks.

S = shuffle.

Refer to "Making the Blocks, Stack the Deck Style" on page 11 for guidance as needed. These blocks are shuffled using the controlled shuffling technique described on page 14. If you are using a cutting template, use the whole-segment template technique described on page 12.

1. Arrange the 5" x 7¾" assorted batik rectangles into 30 decks of four rectangles each, right sides up, alternating the light and medium fabrics. Each deck should contain a different mix of fabrics. Secure each deck with a pin through all the layers.

2. Divide the decks into two sets of 15 decks each. Working with one deck at a time, cut and shuffle the pieces as shown in the appropriate diagram above. Cut one set of 15 decks with a very slight wiggly line from the lower-right to the upper-left corner and the remaining set with a very slight wiggly line from the lower-left to the upper-right corner. Begin and end each cut ¼" from the corner as shown. As you go, secure each deck to a piece of paper by pinning through all the layers.

MAKING THE BLOCKS

Referring to "Sewing the Blocks" on page 15, "Sewing Curves" on page 16, and the diagrams below, sew two segments together as shown; press. Trim the blocks to 4½" x 6¾", making sure the diagonal seam runs from corner to corner. Make 120 blocks—60 with the diagonal seam running from upper left to lower right and 60 with the diagonal seam running from upper right to lower left.

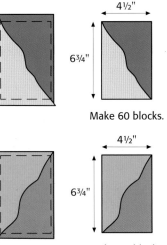

Make 60 blocks.

Make 60 blocks.

ASSEMBLING THE QUILT TOP

Refer to "Assembling the Quilt Top" on page 6 for guidance as needed.

1. Arrange the blocks into 10 vertical rows of 12 blocks each, rotating the blocks so that the lighter fabrics come together to form wiggly diamonds as shown in the quilt photo on page 30. Make sure identical prints aren't touching in the finished layout. View your arrangement through a door peephole (see "The 10-Foot Rule" on page 11) to check the color and block balance.

2. Sew four blocks together, two blocks across by two blocks down, to make a jumbo-sized block. Make 30, pressing as shown.

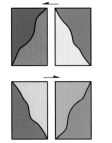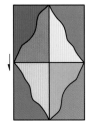

Make 30.

3. Pin and sew the jumbo-sized blocks into six vertical rows of five blocks each as shown in the assembly diagram below; press.

4. Pin and sew the rows from step 3 together in pairs; press.

5. Pin and sew the pairs together; press, re-pressing any seams as needed to make construction easier.

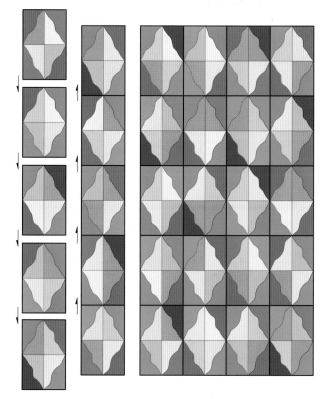

Assembly diagram

ADDING THE BORDERS

1. Refer to "Adding Borders" on page 6. Sew the 1½"-wide light green strips together end to end to make one long inner-border strip.

2. Measure the length of the quilt top through the center and cut two inner-border strips to this measurement. Pin and sew the borders to the sides of the quilt. Press the seams toward the border strips. Measure the width of the quilt top through the center, including the borders just added, and cut two inner-border strips to this measurement. Pin and sew the borders to the top and bottom of the quilt; press.

3. Repeat steps 1 and 2 using the 6"-wide purple print strips to make and attach the outer border.

FINISHING

Refer to "Finishing the Quilt" on page 7 as needed.

1. Divide the backing fabric crosswise into two equal panels, each approximately 86" long. Remove the selvages and sew the pieces together along the long edges to make a backing piece approximately 80" x 86"; press. Trim the backing to 2" to 3" larger than the quilt top all around.

2. Layer the quilt top with the batting and backing, keeping the backing seam parallel to the long edges of the quilt top. Baste the layers together using your favorite method.

3. Hand or machine quilt as desired.

4. Trim the backing and batting even with the edges of the quilt top and use the 2½"-wide strips to bind the quilt.

Quilt plan

QUILTING SUGGESTIONS

I free-motion quilted squiggly lines diagonally through all the blocks in both directions and finished with overall stipple quilting in the border.

Scrap Renovation

Finished Quilt: 64¼" x 89¾"

Finished Block: 9" x 9"

This quilt was designed especially with your stash in mind. It's all about your fabric scraps, leftovers, bits and pieces, remnants, or whatever it is you call your pieces of "saved" fabrics. Give it a try and you'll be amazed at just how big a quilt you can make—and how little your stash is reduced!

FABRIC TIPS

The only fabric purchase I made for this quilt was the backing—all the rest came from my stash. I pulled together six different color groups of 10 fabrics each. Most appear as solids from a distance without any white background. I used "The 10-Foot Rule" (page 11) to pare down the final selection.

MATERIALS

All yardages are based on 42"-wide fabric.

1 square, 12" x 12", *each* of 10 assorted purple, 10 red, 10 blue, 10 tan to gold, 10 light brown to khaki green, and 10 light to medium green prints (60 squares total) for blocks

3 squares, 14" x 14", in coordinating fabric for right- and left-edge setting triangles

10 squares, 7¼" x 7¼", in coordinating fabric for top- and bottom-edge and corner setting triangles

⅔ yard of fabric for binding

5⅓ yards of fabric for backing

69" x 95" piece of batting

Freezer paper

CUTTING

Cut all strips across the fabric width (cross grain).

From the 14" coordinating squares, cut:

Each square diagonally from corner to corner in both directions to yield 4 quarter-square triangles (12 total)

From the 7¼" coordinating squares, cut:

Each square diagonally from corner to corner in one direction to yield 2 half-square triangles (20 total)

From the binding fabric, cut:

8 strips, 2½" x 42"

Block Cutting, Shuffling, and Sewing Guide

Cut Size: 12" x 12"

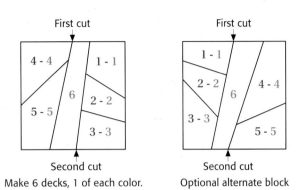

First cut

4 - 4		1 - 1
5 - 5	6	2 - 2
		3 - 3

Second cut

Make 6 decks, 1 of each color.

First cut

	1 - 1	
2 - 2		4 - 4
3 - 3	6	
		5 - 5

Second cut

Optional alternate block

Refer to "Making the Blocks, Stack the Deck Style" on page 11 for guidance as needed. These blocks are cut using a variation of the chipped template method (page 12) and shuffled using the traditional shuffling technique described on page 14.

1. Arrange the ten 12" assorted purple squares right sides up to make a deck. Repeat to make a separate deck for each of the other five colors of 12" squares for a total of six decks. Secure each deck with a pin through all the layers.

2. Refer to the diagrams above and duplicate the drawings on 12" squares of freezer paper. Use scissors to cut each template apart on the drawn lines.

3. Separate the purple deck into two sets of five layers each. Reassemble one template, shiny side down, on top of one purple deck. Use a hot, dry iron to press the paper pieces in place. Cut the fabric deck apart along the cut lines of the templates.

4. Carefully remove the templates and replace them in order on the top of the remaining purple deck; press and cut. Restack the two purple decks, matching all cut lines. Secure each deck with a pin through all the layers.

5. Repeat steps 3 and 4 using the 12" red, blue, tan to gold, light brown to khaki green, and light to medium green decks and either template.

6. Working with one deck at a time, shuffle the pieces as shown in the appropriate diagram above. As you go, secure each deck to a piece of paper by pinning through all the layers.

MAKING THE BLOCKS

1. Referring to "Sewing the Blocks" on page 15 and the diagrams at left and below, sew the shuffled segments for each block together using the chain-piecing technique. Press the seams to one side. Make 60. Trim the blocks to 10½" x 10½".

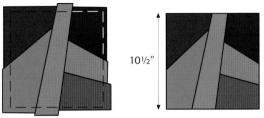

10½"

Make 60 blocks.

2. Slice each block from corner to corner in one direction, creating two half-square triangles. Make 120.

3. Randomly sew a purple, red, or blue half-square triangle together with a tan/gold, brown/khaki, or green half-square triangle; press. Retrim each block to 9½" x 9½". Make 59. (You'll have two half-square triangles left over. Set these aside for another project.)

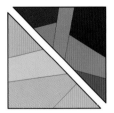 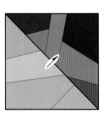

Make 59.

ASSEMBLING THE QUILT TOP

Refer to "Assembling the Quilt Top" on page 6 for guidance as needed.

1. Piece two 7¼" half-square triangles together to make the top and bottom setting triangles; press. Make eight. You'll have four triangles left over. Set these aside for the corner setting triangles.

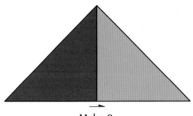

Make 8.

2. Arrange the blocks into 11 diagonal rows as shown in the assembly diagram at right. Place the pieced top and bottom setting triangles from step 1 and the 14" quarter-square right and left setting triangles. Place a remaining 7¼" half-square triangle in each corner. Move the blocks around until you are satisfied with your layout. View your arrangement through a door peephole (see "The 10-Foot Rule" on page 11) to check the color and block balance.

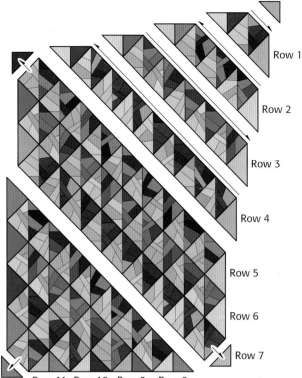

Row 1
Row 2
Row 3
Row 4
Row 5
Row 6
Row 7
Row 11 Row 10 Row 9 Row 8

SETTING SUGGESTION

I laid out my blocks in diagonal rows based on color; that is, a purple row, a red row, and so on, turning the blocks so that the defining color faced the right edge of the quilt.

3. Pin and sew the blocks and side setting triangles together into diagonal rows; press.

4. Pin and sew the rows together as follows: rows 1, 2, 3, and 4; rows 5, 6, and 7; rows 8, 9, 10, and 11. Press the seams to one side.

5. Pin and sew the sections from step 4 together; press.

6. Add the four corner triangles. Press the seams toward the corner triangles.

FINISHING

Refer to "Finishing the Quilt" on page 7 as needed.

1. Divide the backing fabric crosswise into two equal panels, each approximately 96" long. Remove the selvages and sew the pieces together along the long edges to make a backing piece approximately 80" x 96"; press.

2. Layer the quilt top with the batting and backing, keeping the backing seam parallel to the long edges of the quilt top. Baste the layers together using your favorite method.

3. Hand or machine quilt as desired.

4. Trim the backing and batting even with the edges of the quilt top and use the 2½"-wide strips to bind the quilt.

QUILTING SUGGESTIONS

For this quilt, I dropped the feed dogs on my sewing machine and quilted a wiggly line diagonally through the center of each row in both directions.

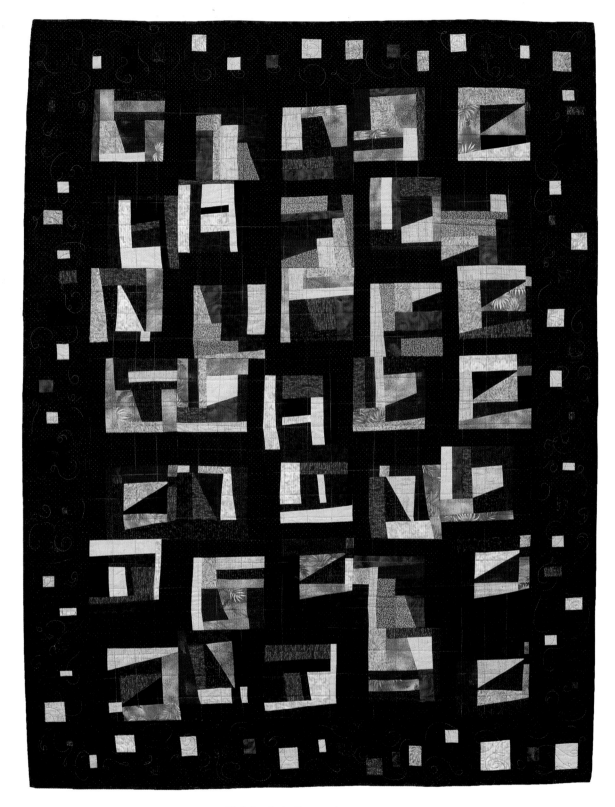

Finished Quilt: 52½" x 68½"

Finished Block: 8" x 8"

The blocks in this quilt were made by repeating some fabrics. Then all the blocks were partially bordered with the same black fabric. The resulting pattern makes it difficult to find the original block.

FABRIC TIP

Choose bright contrasting prints without a lot of pattern so that they appear as solid fabrics from a distance.

MATERIALS

All yardages are based on 42"-wide fabric.

2⅝ yards of black dotted print for blocks and border

3 yards *total* of prints in assorted colors (for example, turquoise, green, red, bluish violet, purple, yellow, gold, orange, and black) for blocks and border

⅝ yard of fabric for binding

3¼ yards of fabric for backing

58" x 74" piece of batting

CUTTING

Cut all strips across the fabric width (cross grain).

From the prints in assorted colors, cut a *total* of:

35 squares, 9½" x 9½"

5 strips, 2" x 12"

4 strips, 1½" x 12"

1 strip, 1" x 12"

2 strips, 2½" x 12"

From the black dotted print, cut:

16 strips, 2" x 42"; crosscut into:

    35 strips, 2" x 7"

    35 strips, 2" x 8½"

11 strips, 2½" x 42"; crosscut into 66 strips, 2½" x 6½"

8 strips, 2½" x 12"

6 strips, 3" x 12"

9 strips, 3½" x 12"

1 strip, 4½" x 12"

From the binding fabric, cut:

7 strips, 2½" x 42"

Block Cutting, Shuffling, and Sewing Guide

Cut Size: 9½" x 9½"

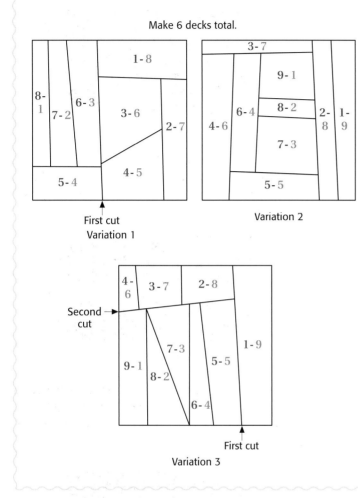

Make 6 decks total.

First cut
Variation 1

Variation 2

Second cut

First cut

Variation 3

Refer to "Making the Blocks, Stack the Deck Style" on page 11 for guidance as needed. These blocks are cut using the chipped template method (page 12). There are three different variations for you to work with in any combination you wish. The blocks are shuffled using the traditional shuffling technique described on page 14.

1. Layer the 9½" assorted print squares into five decks of six squares each and one deck of five squares, right sides up, alternating contrasting colors. In several decks, duplicate one fabric so that it appears in the deck twice. Secure each deck with a pin through all the layers.

2. Working with one deck at a time, cut and shuffle the pieces as shown in the appropriate diagram at left. As you go, secure each deck to a piece of paper by pinning through all the layers.

MAKING THE BLOCKS

1. Referring to "Sewing the Blocks" on page 15 and the diagrams above and below, sew the shuffled segments for each block together. Press the seams to one side. Trim the blocks to 7" x 7". Make 35.

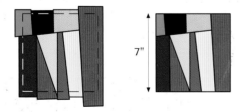

2. Sew a 2" x 7" black dotted strip to the bottom of each block from step 1; press. Sew a 2" x 8½" black dotted strip to the left side; press.

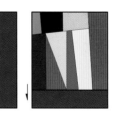

Make 35 blocks total.

ASSEMBLING THE QUILT TOP

Refer to "Assembling the Quilt Top" on page 6 for guidance as needed.

1. Arrange the blocks into five vertical rows of seven blocks each as shown in the assembly diagram below. Move, turn, and mix the blocks until you are satisfied with the arrangement. I purposely placed identical prints side by side to make it difficult to see where the blocks start and end. View your arrangement through a door peephole (see "The 10-Foot Rule" on page 11) to check the color and block balance.

2. Pin and sew the blocks into five vertical rows; press.

3. Pin and sew the rows from step 2 together in pairs; press. Sew the last row to the second pair; press.

4. Pin and sew the units from step 3 together; press.

Assembly diagram

PIECING THE BORDER

1. Sew a 1" x 12" assorted print strip between a 2½" x 12" black dotted strip and a 4½" x 12" black dotted strip to make a strip set as shown; press.

2½"
1"
4½"

Make 1.

2. Sew a 1½" x 12" assorted print strip between a 3½" x 12" black dotted strip and a 3" x 12" black dotted strip to make a strip set as shown; press. Make four.

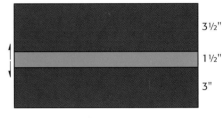

3½"
1½"
3"

Make 4 total.

3. Sew a 2" x 12" assorted print strip between a 2½" x 12" black dotted strip and a 3½" x 12" black dotted strip to make a strip set as shown; press. Make five.

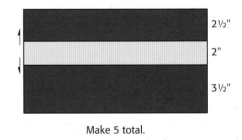

2½"
2"
3½"

Make 5 total.

4. Sew a 2½" x 12" assorted print strip between a 2½" x 12" black dotted strip and a 3" x 12" black dotted strip to make a strip set as shown; press. Make two.

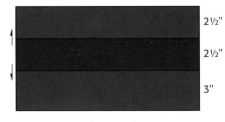

2½"
2½"
3"

Make 2 total.

5. Crosscut each strip set from steps 1–4 into segments, varying the cuts from 1½" to 3" wide. The number isn't important; you've made enough strip sets to achieve the desired border length.

6. Randomly arrange the segments from step 5 so that the same colors are not side by side. Insert a 2½" x 6½" black dotted strip between each segment. (Cut additional 2½" x 6½" strips if needed.) Sew the strips and segments together to create one strip approximately 220" long. Press the seams toward the spacer strips. Straighten the long edges of the unit so that it measures approximately 6½" wide.

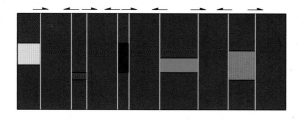

ADDING THE BORDER

Refer to "Adding Borders" on page 6. Measure the length of the quilt top through the center and cut two pieced-border strips (from the unit created in step 6 above) to this measurement. Pin and sew the borders to the sides of the quilt. Press the seams toward the border strips. Measure the width of the quilt top through the center, including the borders just added, and cut two pieced-border strips to this measurement. Pin and sew the borders to the top and bottom of the quilt; press.

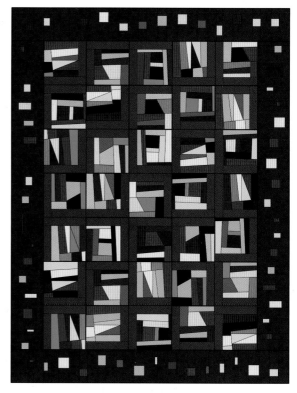

Quilt plan

FINISHING

Refer to "Finishing the Quilt" on page 7 as needed.

1. Divide the backing fabric crosswise into two equal panels, each approximately 58" long. Remove the selvages and sew the pieces together along the long edges to make a backing piece approximately 58" x 80"; press.

2. Layer the quilt top with the batting and backing, keeping the backing seam parallel to the short edges of the quilt top. Baste the layers together using your favorite method.

3. Hand or machine quilt as desired.

4. Trim the backing and batting even with the edges of the quilt top and use the 2½"-wide binding strips to bind the quilt.

QUILTING SUGGESTIONS

I machine quilted a 2" grid across the entire quilt top with variegated thread. For the border, I again used variegated thread to quilt an overall whimsical free-form design.

Browsing the Web

Finished Quilt: 49½" x 68½"
Finished Block: 9½" x 9½"

OK, so what happens when a sweet quilt of posies just doesn't seem to fit the occasion? Try "Browsing the Web"—it's a fun and easy quilt to make and is right on the edge of wacky. Enjoy!

FABRIC TIPS

I chose a variety of light gray, brown, tan, peach, and purple prints that appear as solids from a distance. Light-value batiks also work well.

MATERIALS

All yardages are based on 42"-wide fabric.

1 yard of gray fabric for outer border

½ yard *each* of light yellow, light blue, light purple, and light peach fabric for blocks

½ yard *each* of 2 different light brown and 2 light gray prints for blocks (4 fabrics total)

⅓ yard of black fabric for inner border

¼ yard *each* of 3 black fabrics for spiders

Assorted scraps of red fabrics for rosebuds

Assorted scraps of green and brown fabrics for rosebud cups (calyxes), leaves, and stems

⅝ yard of fabric for binding

3⅛ yards of fabric for backing

55" x 74" piece of batting

1½ yards of fusible web

CUTTING

Cut all strips across the fabric width (cross grain).

From e*ach* light fabric (8 fabrics total), cut:

1 strip, 12½" x 42"; crosscut into 3 squares, 12½" x 12½" (24 total)

From the black inner-border fabric, cut:

5 strips, 1½" x 42"

From the gray outer-border fabric, cut:

6 strips, 5" x 42"

From the binding fabric, cut:

7 strips, 2½" x 42"

Block Cutting, Shuffling, and Sewing Guide

Cut Size: 12½" x 12½"

First cuts

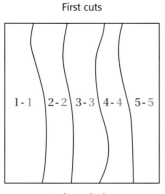

Make 4 decks.

Second cuts

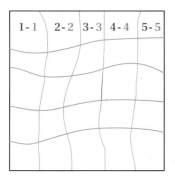

Refer to "Making the Blocks, Stack the Deck Style" on page 11 for guidance as needed. These blocks are shuffled using the traditional shuffling technique described on page 14. If you are using a cutting template, use the whole-segment template technique described on page 12.

1. Arrange the 12½" assorted light squares into four decks of six squares each, right sides up, alternating fabrics. Each deck should contain a different mix of fabrics. Secure each deck with a pin through all the layers.

2. Working with one deck at a time, cut and shuffle the pieces as shown in the first cuts diagram above. As you go, secure each deck to a piece of paper by pinning through all the layers.

MAKING THE BLOCKS

1. Referring to "Sewing the Blocks" on page 15, "Sewing the Curves" on page 16, and the first cuts diagram at left, sew the shuffled segments for each block together with the chain-piecing technique. Press the seams to one side. Make 24.

2. Press the blocks from step 1 and restack. Turn the blocks 90°. Crosscut, shuffle, and chain piece the blocks as shown in the second cuts diagram at left; press. If necessary, trim the blocks to 10" x 10". It's fine if your blocks are smaller or larger; just trim them all to the same size.

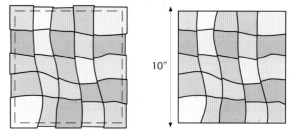

Make 24 blocks.

ASSEMBLING THE QUILT TOP

Refer to "Assembling the Quilt Top" on page 6 for guidance as needed.

1. Arrange the blocks into four vertical rows of six blocks each as shown in the assembly diagram on page 46. Move, turn, and mix the blocks until you are satisfied with the arrangement. (It's OK if a few prints end up side by side.) View your arrangement through a door peephole (see "The 10-Foot Rule" on page 11) to check the color and block balance.

2. Pin and sew the blocks into four vertical rows; press.

3. Pin and sew the rows from step 2 together in pairs; press.

4. Pin and sew the pairs together; press.

Assembly diagram

ADDING THE BORDERS

1. Refer to "Adding Borders" on page 6. Sew the 1½"-wide black strips together end to end to make one long inner-border strip.

2. Measure the length of the quilt top through the center and cut two inner-border strips to this measurement. Pin and sew the borders to the sides of the quilt. Press the seams toward the border strips. Measure the width of the quilt top through the center, including the borders just added, and cut two inner-border strips to this measurement. Pin and sew the borders to the top and bottom of the quilt; press.

3. Repeat steps 1 and 2 with the 5"-wide gray strips to make and attach the outer border.

ADDING THE APPLIQUÉS

1. Referring to "Fusible-Web Appliqué" on page 5, use the patterns on pages 47–48 and the ¼ yard cuts of three black fabrics to prepare a total of eight spiders for fusing and the assorted red, green, and brown scraps to prepare 10 rosebuds and rosebud cups (calyxes), 36 leaves, and nine stems.

2. Referring to the quilt photo on page 43, position and fuse the prepared appliqués to the quilt top. Use your favorite method to stitch around the outer edges of the shapes. I used a straight stitch just inside the edges.

FINISHING

Refer to "Finishing the Quilt" on page 7 as needed.

1. Divide the backing fabric crosswise into two equal panels, each approximately 56" long. Remove the selvages and sew the pieces together along the long edges to make a backing piece approximately 56" x 80"; press.

2. Layer the quilt top with the batting and backing, keeping the backing seam parallel to the short edges of the quilt top. Baste the layers together using your favorite method.

3. Hand or machine quilt as desired.

4. Trim the backing and batting even with the edges of the quilt top and use the 2½"-wide strips to bind the quilt.

Quilt plan

Pattern is full-sized and does not include seam allowance. Pattern is reversed for fusible appliqué.

Patterns are full-sized and do not include seam allowances. Patterns are reversed for fusible appliqué.

Cut 10.   Cut 10.

Cut 10.

Cut 36.

← Cut 9 stems, 13" long.

Bingo

Finished Quilt: 39½" x 51½"

Finished Block: 6" x 6"

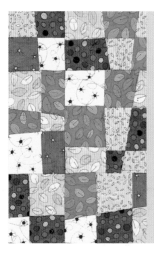

Here's a traditional pattern with a twist. This quilt was originally created so that the blocks would alternate with one another and be finished with a traditional solid border. However, it was soon obvious that the design was everything but traditional and that is when the separation took place. The Nine Patch blocks gathered in the center, the Hourglass blocks moved to the border, and "Bingo" is the result.

FABRIC TIPS

For a whimsical feel, I chose bright turquoise and yellow prints for the Nine Patch blocks and black-and-white polka dots for the Hourglass border blocks.

MATERIALS

All yardages are based on 42"-wide fabric.

⅞ yard *each* of a black-with-white polka dot and a white-with-black polka dot for Hourglass border blocks and cornerstones

⅓ yard *each* of 3 assorted bright turquoise and bright yellow prints for Nine Patch blocks (6 fabrics total)

½ yard of yellowish green fabric for inner border

½ yard of fabric for binding

2⅝ yards of fabric for backing

45" x 56" piece of batting

CUTTING

Cut all strips across the fabric width (cross grain).

From *each* bright turquoise and yellow print, cut:

1 strip, 8" x 42"; crosscut into 4 squares, 8" x 8" (24 total)

From the black-with-white polka dot, cut:

3 strips, 8" x 42"; crosscut into 12 squares, 8" x 8"

4 squares, 2" x 2"

From the white-with-black polka dot, cut:

3 strips, 8" x 42"; crosscut into 12 squares, 8" x 8"

From the yellowish green fabric, cut:

4 strips, 2" x 42"; crosscut into:
    2 strips, 2" x 24½"
    2 strips, 2" x 36½"

2 strips, 2" x 42"; crosscut into 8 pieces, 2" x 6½"

From the binding fabric, cut:

5 strips, 2½" x 42"

Block Cutting, Shuffling, and Sewing Guide

Cut Size: 8" x 8"

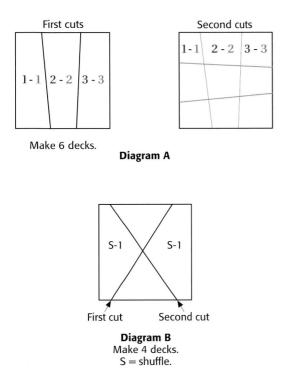

First cuts

1 - 1 | 2 - 2 | 3 - 3

Make 6 decks.

Diagram A

Second cuts

1 - 1 | 2 - 2 | 3 - 3

S-1 | S-1

First cut   Second cut

Diagram B
Make 4 decks.
S = shuffle.

Refer to "Making the Blocks, Stack the Deck Style" on page 11 for guidance as needed. These Nine Patch blocks are shuffled using the traditional shuffling technique described on page 14. The Hourglass blocks are shuffled using the controlled shuffling technique described on page 14. If you are using a cutting template, use a whole-segment template as described on page 12 for the Nine Patch blocks and a chipped template as described on page 12 for the Hourglass blocks.

1. Arrange the 8" yellow and turquoise squares into four decks of six squares each, right sides up, alternating colors. Each deck should contain a different mix of fabrics. Secure each deck with a pin through all the layers.

2. Working with one deck at a time, cut and shuffle the pieces as shown in the first cuts diagram in diagram A at left. Skew some of the cuts a little so that the blocks are different from one another. As you finish each deck, secure it to a piece of paper by pinning through all the layers.

3. Arrange the 8" black-and-white squares and white-and-black squares into four decks of six squares each, right sides up, alternating black with white. Secure each deck with a pin through all the layers.

4. Referring to diagram B, repeat step 2 with the decks from step 3.

MAKING THE NINE PATCH BLOCKS

1. Referring to "Sewing the Blocks" on page 15 and the first cuts diagram in diagram A above, sew the shuffled segments for each block together using the chain-piecing technique. Press the seams to one side. Make 24.

2. Press the blocks from step 1 and restack. Turn the blocks 90°. Crosscut, shuffle, and chain piece the blocks as shown in the second cuts diagram in diagram A above; press. Trim the blocks to 6½" x 6½". Make 24.

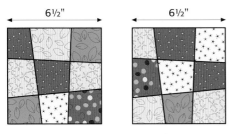

6½"   6½"

Make 12 blocks of each.

MAKING THE HOURGLASS BLOCKS

Referring to "Sewing the Blocks" on page 15, diagram B above, and the diagram below, sew the shuffled segments for each block together as shown. Begin by sewing the segments into pairs; press. Sew the pairs together; press. Trim the blocks to 6½" x 6½". Make 24.

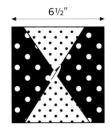

6½"

Make 24 blocks.

ASSEMBLING THE QUILT TOP

Refer to "Assembling the Quilt Top" on page 6 for guidance as needed.

1. Arrange the Nine Patch blocks into four vertical rows of six blocks each as shown in the assembly diagram below, positioning the blocks so that the blocks with dark corners alternate with the blocks with light corners. Move, turn, and mix the blocks until you are satisfied with the arrangement. View your arrangement through a door peephole (see "The 10-Foot Rule" on page 11) to check the color and block balance.

2. Pin and sew the blocks into vertical rows; press.

3. Pin and sew the rows from step 2 together in pairs; press.

4. Pin and sew the pairs together; press.

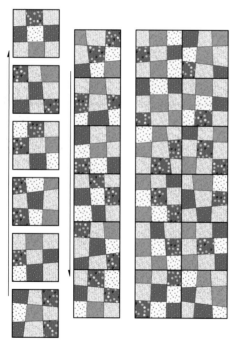

Assembly diagram

ADDING THE BORDERS

1. Sew four Hourglass blocks together to make a row, taking care to orient the blocks as shown; press. Make two.

Make 2.

2. Repeat step 1 but use six Hourglass blocks and orient them as shown; press. Make two.

Make 2.

3. Referring to the quilt plan on page 53, sew a 2" x 36½" yellowish green strip to one long edge of each unit from step 2. Press the seams toward the strip. Sew a unit to the right and left sides of the quilt top; press.

4. Referring to the quilt plan, sew a 2" x 6½" yellowish green strip and a 2" black-and-white square to each end of a 2" x 24½" yellowish green strip; press. Make two.

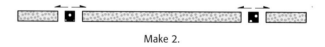

Make 2.

5. Referring to the quilt plan, sew a 2" x 6½" yellowish green strip and a remaining Hourglass block to each end of a unit from step 1; press. Make two.

Make 2.

6. Sew a unit from step 4 and a unit from step 5 to the top and bottom of the quilt; press.

Quilt plan

FINISHING

Refer to "Finishing the Quilt" on page 7 as needed.

1. Divide the backing fabric crosswise into two equal panels, each approximately 47" long. Remove the selvages and sew the pieces together along the long edges to make a backing piece approximately 47" x 80"; press. Trim the backing to 2" to 3" larger than the quilt top all around.

2. Layer the quilt top with the batting and backing, keeping the backing seam parallel to the short edges of the quilt top. Baste the layers together using your favorite method.

3. Hand or machine quilt as desired.

4. Trim the backing and batting even with the edges of the quilt top and use the 2½"-wide strips to bind the quilt.

QUILTING SUGGESTIONS

I quilted an overall, whimsical stipple design throughout the Nine Patch and Hourglass blocks. For the inner border, I added a straight line of quilting ¼" from the inner and outer seams.

Marble Parquet

Finished Quilt: 55½" x 71½"

Finished Block: 5" x 6"

While visiting my brother in California, we toured a historic house in Malibu. The awesome floors with patterns of inlaid marble were the inspiration for this quilt.

MATERIALS

All yardages are based on 42"-wide fabric.

⅝ yard *each* of 8 assorted light batiks for blocks

⅓ yard *each* of 5 assorted burgundy batiks for blocks

⅔ yard of medium purple fabric for border

⅝ yard of fabric for binding

3⅓ yards of fabric for backing

60" x 76" piece of batting

CUTTING

Cut all strips across the fabric width (cross grain).

From *each* light batik, cut:

2 strips, 7½" x 42"; crosscut into 11 rectangles, 6½" x 7½" (88 total; you will use 87)

From *each* burgundy batik, cut:

1 strip, 7½" x 42; crosscut into 5 rectangles, 6½" x 7½" (25 total)

From the purple fabric, cut:

7 strips, 3" x 42"

From the binding fabric, cut:

7 strips, 2½" x 42"

Block Cutting, Shuffling, and Sewing Guide

Cut Size: 6½" x 7½"

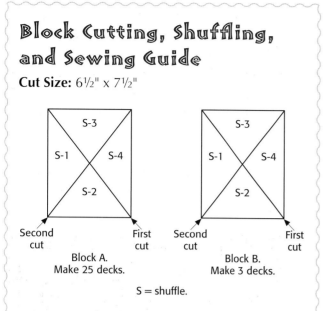

Block A.
Make 25 decks.

Block B.
Make 3 decks.

S = shuffle.

Refer to "Making the Blocks, Stack the Deck Style" on page 11 for guidance as needed. These blocks are shuffled using the traditional shuffling technique described on page 14. If you are using a cutting template, use the chipped template technique described on page 12.

1. Stack three 6½" x 7½" assorted light rectangles and one 6½" x 7½" burgundy rectangle right sides up to make a deck. Make 25 decks with the burgundy rectangle always on top. Secure each deck with a pin through all the layers and label these block A. Stack the remaining light rectangles into three decks of four rectangles each and label these block B.

2. Working with one deck at a time, cut and shuffle the pieces as shown in the diagrams for blocks and A and B above. As you go, secure each deck to a piece of paper by pinning through all the layers.

MAKING THE BLOCKS

Referring to "Sewing the Blocks" on page 15 and the diagrams above and at right, sew the shuffled segments for each block together one block at a time as shown; press. Begin by sewing the segments together into pairs; press. Sew the pairs together by matching the center seams and then twisting the top layer a bit until the raw

edges line up; press. Trim the block to 5½" x 6½". Make 100 A blocks and 12 B blocks. (The dark triangle will rotate around the block in block A.)

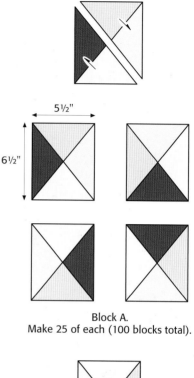

Block A.
Make 25 of each (100 blocks total).

Block B.
Make 12 blocks.

ASSEMBLING THE QUILT TOP

Refer to "Assembling the Quilt Top" on page 6 for guidance as needed.

1. Arrange the blocks into 10 vertical rows of 11 blocks each, carefully placing and turning the A blocks as shown in the assembly diagram on page 57. (You will have two A blocks left over. Set these aside for another project.) Move the blocks until you are satisfied with the arrangement. Make sure identical prints are not touching in the finished layout. View your arrangement through a door peephole (see "The 10-Foot Rule" on page 11) to check the color and block balance.

2. Pin and sew the blocks into vertical rows; press.

3. Pin and sew the rows from step 2 together in pairs; press.

4. Pin and sew the pairs together; press.

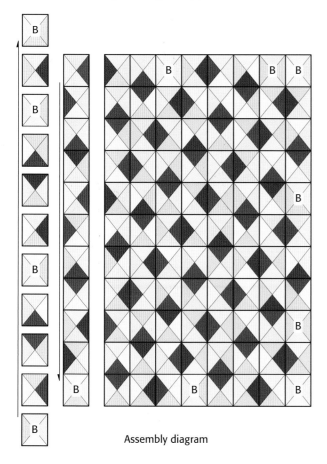

Assembly diagram

ADDING THE BORDERS

1. Refer to "Adding Borders" on page 6. Sew the 3"-wide purple strips together end to end to make one long border strip.

2. Measure the length of the quilt top through the center and cut two border strips to this measurement. Pin and sew the borders to the sides of the quilt. Press the seams toward the border strips. Measure the width of the quilt top through the center, including the borders just added, and cut two border strips to this measurement. Pin and sew the borders to the top and bottom of the quilt; press.

FINISHING

Refer to "Finishing the Quilt" on page 7 as needed.

1. Divide the backing fabric crosswise into two equal panels, each approximately 60" long. Remove the selvages and sew the pieces together along the long edges to make a backing piece approximately 60" x 80"; press.

2. Layer the quilt top with the batting and backing, keeping the backing seam parallel to the short edges of the quilt top. Baste the layers together using your favorite method.

3. Hand or machine quilt as desired.

4. Trim the backing and batting even with the edges of the quilt top and use the 2½"-wide strips to bind the quilt.

Quilt plan

QUILTING SUGGESTIONS

I quilted in the ditch to anchor the vertical and horizontal seams and diagonally in both directions in the blocks. I finished with light overall stipple quilting in the borders.

Diamond Throw

Finished Quilt: 58½" x 72½"

Finished Block: 5½" x 7¼"

This is a fun, fast, and easy quilt to make for a quick gift or seasonal throw. The variety of fabrics creates a cozy patchwork effect.

MATERIALS

All yardages are based on 42"-wide fabric.

1¼ yards of red print for outer border

¼ yard *each* of 6 assorted dark and 6 assorted light prints for blocks (12 fabrics total)

⅓ yard of black fabric for inner border

⅝ yard of fabric for binding

3⅝ yards of fabric for backing

64" x 78" piece of batting

CUTTING

Cut all strips across the fabric width (cross grain).

From the assorted dark fabrics, cut a *total* of:

32 rectangles, 6½" x 8½"

From the assorted light fabrics, cut a *total* of:

32 rectangles, 6½" x 8½"

From the black fabric, cut:

6 strips, 1½" x 42"

From the red print, cut:

6 strips, 6½" x 42"

From the binding fabric, cut:

7 strips, 2½" x 42"

Block Cutting, Shuffling, and Sewing Guide

Cut Size: 6½" x 8½"

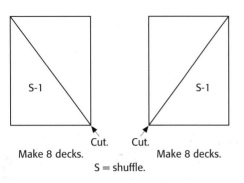

S-1

S-1

Cut.   Cut.

Make 8 decks.   Make 8 decks.

S = shuffle.

Refer to "Making the Blocks, Stack the Deck Style" on page 11 for guidance as needed. These blocks are shuffled using the controlled shuffling technique described on page 14. If you are using a cutting template, use the whole-segment template technique described on page 12.

1. Arrange the 6½" x 8½" assorted dark and light rectangles into 16 decks of four rectangles each, right sides up, alternating the light and dark fabrics. Each deck should contain a different mix of fabrics. Secure each deck with a pin through all the layers.

2. Divide the decks into two sets of eight decks each. Working with one deck at a time, cut and shuffle the pieces as shown in the appropriate diagram above. Cut one set of eight decks diagonally from the lower-right to the upper-left corner and the remaining set from the lower-left to the upper-right corner as shown. As you go, secure each deck to a piece of paper by pinning through all the layers.

MAKING THE BLOCKS

Referring to "Sewing the Blocks" on page 15 and the diagrams below, sew two segments together using the chain-piecing technique; press. Trim the blocks to 5½" x 7¾", making sure the diagonal seam runs from corner to corner. Make 64 blocks—32 with the diagonal seam running in one direction and 32 with the diagonal seam running in the opposite direction.

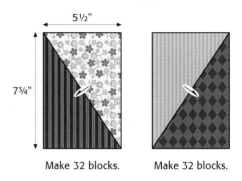

Make 32 blocks.   Make 32 blocks.

ASSEMBLING THE QUILT TOP

Refer to "Assembling the Quilt Top" on page 6 for guidance as needed.

1. Arrange the blocks into eight vertical rows of eight blocks each, rotating the blocks so that the darker fabrics come together to form diamonds as shown in the quilt photo on page 58. Move the blocks until you are satisfied with the arrangement. Make sure identical prints are not touching in the finished layout. View your arrangement through a door peephole (see "The 10-Foot Rule" on page 11) to check the color and block balance.

2. Sew four blocks together, two blocks across by two blocks down, to make a jumbo-sized block. Make 16, pressing the seams as shown.

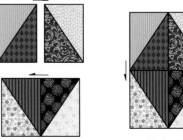

Make 16.

3. Pin and sew the jumbo-sized blocks together into four vertical rows of four blocks each as shown in the assembly diagram on page 61; press.

4. Pin and sew the rows from step 3 together in pairs; press.

5. Pin and sew the pairs together; press, re-pressing the seams as needed to make construction easier.

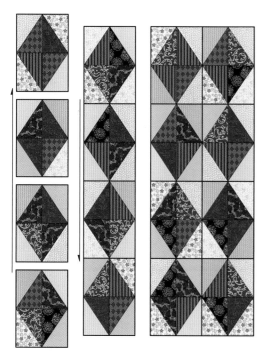

Assembly diagram

ADDING THE BORDERS

1. Refer to "Adding Borders" on page 6. Sew the 1½"-wide black strips together end to end to make one long inner-border strip.

2. Measure the length of the quilt top through the center and cut two border strips to this measurement. Pin and sew the borders to the sides of the quilt. Press the seams toward the border strips. Measure the width of the quilt top through the center, including the borders just added, and cut two border strips to this measurement. Pin and sew the borders to the top and bottom of the quilt; press.

3. Repeat steps 1 and 2 with the 6½"-wide red print strips to make and attach the outer border.

FINISHING

Refer to "Finishing the Quilt" on page 7 as needed.

1. Divide the backing fabric crosswise into two equal panels, each approximately 65" long. Remove the selvages and sew the pieces together along the long edges to make a backing piece approximately 65" x 80"; press.

2. Layer the quilt top with the batting and backing, keeping the backing seam parallel to the short edges of the quilt top. Baste the layers together using your favorite method.

3. Hand or machine quilt as desired.

4. Trim the backing and batting even with the edges of the quilt top and use the 2½"-wide strips to bind the quilt.

Quilt plan

QUILTING SUGGESTIONS

I used a traditional, overall stipple pattern for the blocks and wide outer border. For the inner border, I quilted in the ditch on the inside seam and added straight-line stitching ¼" from the seam closest to the outer border.

The Spin

Finished Quilt: 62" x 82"
Finished Block: 10" x 10"

I created this quilt to showcase all the fascinating large-scale prints now available. This quilt has a veggie theme but any theme will work.

FABRIC TIPS

Look for a fun group of large-scale prints to use for the centers in the spinning blocks. Each block center can be from the same fabric or each one can be different.

MATERIALS

All yardages are based on 42"-wide fabric.

1⅓ yards of purple fabric for inner and outer borders

⅜ yard *each* of 6 assorted feature prints for block centers

⅜ yard *each* of 6 assorted green and tan prints for blocks

⅜ yard *each* of 6 assorted purple and blue prints for blocks

⅜ yard of blue fabric for middle border

⅔ yard of fabric for binding

4⅞ yards of fabric for backing

67" x 87" piece of batting

CUTTING

Cut all strips across the fabric width (cross grain).

From the feature prints, cut a *total* of:

35 squares, 7" x 7"

From *each* purple and blue print, cut:

5 strips, 2¼" x 42" (30 total); crosscut into:
  6 rectangles, 2¼" x 12" (36 total)
  6 rectangles, 2¼" x 14" (36 total)

From *each* green and tan print, cut:

5 strips, 2¼" x 42" (30 total); crosscut into:
  6 rectangles, 2¼" x 12" (36 total)
  6 rectangles, 2¼" x 14" (36 total)

From the purple border fabric, cut:

7 strips, 1¾" x 42"

7 strips, 4" x 42"

From the blue middle-border fabric, cut:

7 strips, 1½" x 42"

From the binding fabric, cut:

8 strips, 2½" x 42"

Block Cutting, Shuffling, and Sewing Guide

Cut Size: 7" x 7"

Refer to "Making the Blocks, Stack the Deck Style" on page 11 for guidance as needed.

1. Separate the 7" feature-print squares into two separate decks: square A with 17 squares and square B with 18 squares. When completed, the blocks will appear to spin differently in the finished quilt, so label the two decks and set them aside, making sure to keep them separate.

2. Arrange the 2¼" x 12" assorted blue and purple rectangles into six decks of six rectangles each, right sides up. Secure each deck with a pin through all the layers.

3. Working with one deck at a time, cut each deck from step 2 from the lower-left corner to the upper-right corner as shown. Pick up the sections on the right side, rotate them 180°, and place them exactly on top of the triangles on the left side. These will be used for round 1; label them A1.

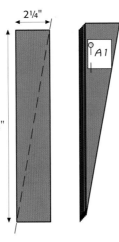

4. Arrange the 2¼" x 14" assorted green and tan rectangles into six decks of six rectangles each, right sides up. Secure each deck with a pin through all the layers.

5. Working with one deck at a time, cut each deck from step 4 from the lower-left corner to the upper-right corner as shown. Pick up the sections on the right side, rotate them 180°, and place them exactly on top of the triangles on the left side. These will be used for round 2; label them A2.

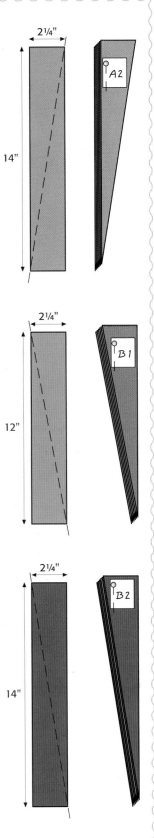

6. Repeat step 2 with the 2¼" x 12" assorted green and tan rectangles. Working with one deck at a time, cut each deck from the lower-right corner to the upper-left corner as shown. Pick up the sections on the left side, rotate them 180°, and place them exactly on top of the triangles on the right side. These will be used for round 1; label them B1.

7. Repeat step 4 with the 2¼" x 14" assorted blue and purple rectangles. Working with one deck at a time, cut each deck from corner to corner from the lower-right corner to the upper-left corner as shown. Pick up the sections on the left side, rotate them 180°, and place them exactly on top of the triangles on the right side. These will be used for round 2; label them B2.

MAKING THE BLOCKS

Refer to "Sewing the Blocks" on page 15. You'll have four triangles left over in each size. Set these aside for another project.

1. You will use the A squares and pieces A1 and A2 to make the A blocks. Align the upper-right corner of a 7" A square, right sides together, with the 90° corner of an A1 triangle as shown. Sew the pieces together, leaving the last 3" of the seam unsewn. Working counterclockwise and aligning the pieces in the same fashion, sew an A1 triangle to the remaining three sides of the A square, this time completing each seam. Return to the first triangle and complete the seam. Press the seams toward the center square. Use scissors to trim the "tails" of the skinny triangles even with the edges of the block.

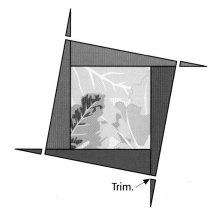

Block A, round 1.
Blue numbers indicate sewing order.

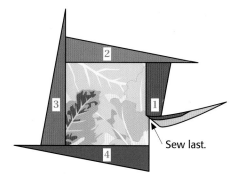

Trim.

2. Repeat step 1 to add the A2 triangles to the unit; press. Make 17 A blocks.

Block A.
Make 17 blocks.

TO TRIM OR NOT TO TRIM

I trimmed all my blocks—A and B—to 10½" x 10½"; however, if your blocks don't need to be squared and are all the same size, you can skip this step. As long as your blocks are square and consistent, you will be fine.

3. You will use the B squares and pieces B1 and B2 to make the B blocks. Align the upper-left corner of a 7" B square, right sides together, with the 90° corner of a B1 triangle. Sew the pieces together, leaving the last 3" of the seam unsewn. Working clockwise and aligning the pieces in the same fashion, sew a B1 triangle to the remaining three sides of the B square, this time completing each seam. Return to the first triangle and complete the seam. Press the seams toward the center square. Use scissors to trim the "tails" of the skinny triangles even with the edges of the block.

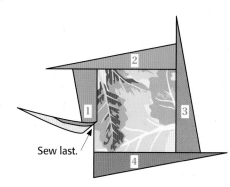

Sew last.

Block B, round 1.
Blue numbers indicate sewing order.

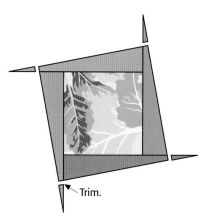

Trim.

4. Repeat step 3 to add the B2 triangles to the unit; press. Make 18 B blocks.

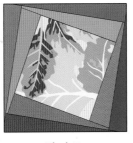

**Block B.
Make 18 blocks.**

ASSEMBLING THE QUILT TOP

Refer to "Assembling the Quilt Top" on page 6 for guidance as needed.

1. Arrange the blocks into five vertical rows of seven blocks each, alternating the A and B blocks as shown in the assembly diagram below. Move the blocks around until you are satisfied with the layout. View your arrangement through a door peephole (see "The 10-Foot Rule" on page 11) to check the color and block balance.

2. Pin and sew the blocks into five vertical rows; press.

3. Pin and sew rows 1, 2, and 3 together; press. Repeat with rows 4 and 5; press.

4. Pin and sew the units from step 3 together; press.

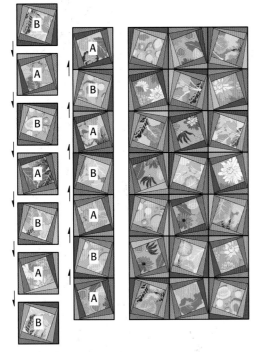

Assembly diagram

ADDING THE BORDERS

1. Refer to "Adding Borders" on page 6. Sew the 1¾"-wide purple strips together end to end to make one long inner-border strip.

2. Measure the length of the quilt top through the center and cut two inner-border strips to this measurement. Pin and sew the borders to the sides of the quilt. Press the seams toward the border strips. Measure the width of the quilt top through the center, including the borders just added, and cut two inner-border strips to this measurement. Pin and sew the borders to the top and bottom of the quilt; press.

3. Repeat steps 1 and 2 with the 1½"-wide blue strips to make and attach the middle border and the 4"-wide purple strips to make and attach the outer border. Press the seams toward each newly added border.

FINISHING

Refer to "Finishing the Quilt" on page 7 as needed.

1. Divide the backing fabric crosswise into two equal panels, each approximately 88" long. Remove the selvages and sew the pieces together along the long edges to make a backing piece approximately 80" x 88"; press. Trim the backing to 2" to 3" larger than the quilt top all around.

2. Layer the quilt top with the batting and backing, keeping the backing seam parallel to the long edges of the quilt top. Baste the layers together using your favorite method.

3. Hand or machine quilt as desired.

4. Trim the backing and batting even with the edges of the quilt top and use the 2½"-wide strips to bind the quilt.

QUILTING SUGGESTIONS

I quilted an overall stipple design for the blocks and middle and outer borders. For the middle blue border, I added a straight line of quilting ¼" from the inner and outer seams.

Finished Quilt: 55½" x 71½"
Finished Block: 6½" x 6½"

In this quilt, warm and cool colors mix together to create kaleidoscope blocks. It's fast and easy, and every block yields a surprise.

FABRIC TIP

I chose a variety of warm- and cool-colored prints for this quilt. Since most are tone-on-tone, they appear as solids from a distance.

MATERIALS

All yardages are based on 42"-wide fabric.

1¼ yards of blue fabric for outer border

¾ yard of black-and-white check for sashing and inner border

⅓ yard *each* of 8 assorted warm colors (for example, yellow, gold, orange, peach, and pink) for blocks

⅓ yard *each* of 8 assorted cool colors (for example, blue, turquoise, and green) for blocks and cornerstones

⅝ yard of fabric for binding

3½ yards of fabric for backing

61" x 77" piece of batting

CUTTING

Cut all strips across the fabric width (cross grain).

From *each* warm- and cool-colored print, cut:

1 strip, 8" x 42"; crosscut into 3 rectangles, 8" x 11½" (48 total)

From 1 cool-colored print, cut:

6 squares, 1½" x 1½"

From a different cool-colored print, cut:

4 squares, 2½" x 2½"

From the black-and-white check, cut:

6 strips, 1½" x 42"; crosscut into 17 strips, 1½" x 12½"
5 strips, 2½" x 42"

From the blue outer-border fabric, cut:

6 strips, 6½" x 42"

From the binding fabric, cut:

7 strips, 2½" x 42"

Block Cutting, Shuffling, and Sewing Guide

Cut Size: 8" x 11½"

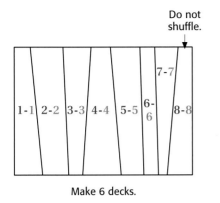

Do not shuffle.

Make 6 decks.

Refer to "Making the Blocks, Stack the Deck Style" on page 11 for guidance as needed. These blocks are shuffled using the traditional shuffling technique described on page 14. If you are using a cutting template, use the whole-segment template technique described on page 12.

1. Arrange the 8" x 11½" rectangles into six decks of eight rectangles each, right sides up, alternating the warm and cool prints. Each deck should contain a different mix of fabrics. Secure each deck with a pin through all the layers.

2. Working with one deck at a time, cut and shuffle the pieces as shown in the diagram above. As you go, secure each deck to a piece of paper by pinning through all the layers.

MAKING THE BLOCKS

1. Referring to "Sewing the Blocks" on page 15 and the diagrams at left and below, sew the shuffled segments for each block together using the chain-piecing technique. Press the seams to one side. Make 48. Trim the blocks to 7½" x 7½".

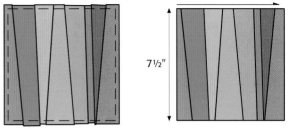

7½"

Make 48 blocks.

2. Divide the blocks into two sets of 24 blocks each. Cut one set of blocks from the lower-left to the upper-right corner to create two half-square triangles. Label these A. Cut the remaining set of blocks from the lower-right to the upper-left corner. Label these B.

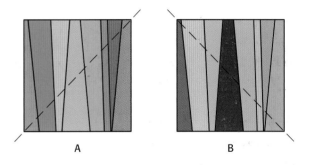

A

B

3. Randomly sew an A half-square triangle together with a B half-square triangle. Press the seams to one side. Retrim each block to 6½" x 6½". Make 48.

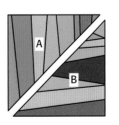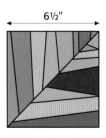

6½"

Make 48.

4. Arrange four blocks from step 3 in two rows of two blocks each as shown. Sew the blocks together in pairs; press. Sew the pairs together; press. Make 12.

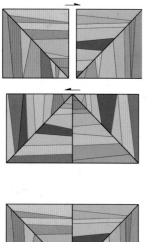

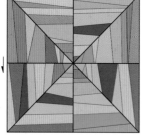

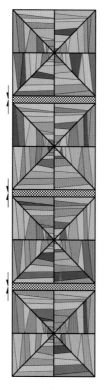

Make 12.

ASSEMBLING THE QUILT TOP

1. Arrange the blocks into three vertical rows of four blocks each as shown in the assembly diagram at far right, leaving space between the blocks for the sashing strips. Once you are satisfied with the layout, add the 1½" x 12½" check sashing strips and 1½"-square cool-colored cornerstones. View your arrangement through a door peephole (see "The 10-Foot Rule" on page 11) to check the color and block balance.

2. Pin and sew the blocks and horizontal sashing strips together into vertical rows. Press the seams toward the sashing strips. Make three rows, replacing them in the layout as you go.

Make 3.

3. Pin and sew the vertical sashing strips and cornerstones together into vertical rows. Press the seams toward the sashing strips. Make two rows, replacing them in the layout as you go.

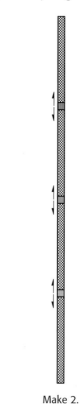

Make 2.

4. Sew the sashing/cornerstone rows from step 3 to the block/sashing rows from step 2. Press the seams toward the sashing/cornerstone rows.

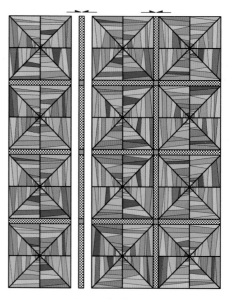

Assembly diagram

ADDING THE BORDERS

1. Refer to "Adding Borders" on page 6. Sew the 2½"-wide check strips together end to end to make one long inner-border strip.

2. Measure the length of the quilt top through the center and cut two inner-border strips to this measurement for the side borders. Measure the width of the quilt top through the center and cut two inner-border strips to this measurement for the top and bottom inner borders.

3. Pin and sew the side inner borders to the sides of the quilt. Press the seam toward the border strips.

4. Sew a 2½" cool-colored square to each short end of the top inner-border strip. Press the seams toward the border strips. Repeat for the bottom strip. Pin and sew to the top and bottom of the quilt; press.

5. Sew the 6½"-wide blue strips together end to end to make one long outer-border strip.

6. Measure the length of the quilt top through the center and cut two outer-border strips to this measurement. Pin and sew the borders to the sides of the quilt. Press the seams toward the border strips. Measure the width of the quilt top through the center, including the borders just added, and cut two outer-border strips to this measurement. Pin and sew the borders to the top and bottom of the quilt; press.

FINISHING

Refer to "Finishing the Quilt" on page 7 as needed.

1. Divide the backing fabric crosswise into two equal panels, each approximately 63" long. Remove the selvages and sew the pieces together along the long edges to make a backing piece approximately 63" x 80"; press.

2. Layer the quilt top with the batting and backing, keeping the backing seam parallel to the short edges of the quilt top. Baste the layers together using your favorite method.

3. Hand or machine quilt as desired.

4. Trim the backing and batting even with the edges of the quilt top and use the 2½"-wide binding strips to bind the quilt.

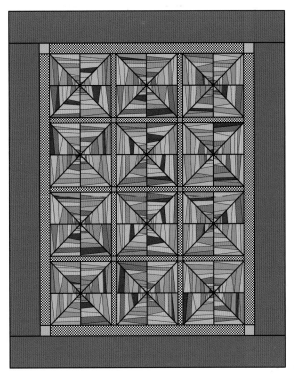

Quilt plan

QUILTING SUGGESTIONS

I quilted in the ditch to anchor the vertical and horizontal seams in the center of the quilt. I quilted diagonally in both directions in the blocks. For the inner border, I quilted in the ditch on the inside seam and added straight-line stitching ¼" from the seam closest to the outer border. I finished with overall stipple quilting in the outer border.

Trident Links

Finished Quilt: 61" x 73"
Finished Block: 6" x 6"

This is a fun block to make—not quite a Nine Patch, but similar. I liked the uneven appearance of the squares linking throughout the quilt top.

MATERIALS

All yardages are based on 42"-wide fabric.

1⅓ yards of purple fabric for outer border

⅝ yard *each* of 8 assorted (for example, tan, light green, yellow, black, brown, dark green, and purple) prints for blocks

⅓ yard of green fabric for inner border

⅝ yard of fabric for binding

3¾ yards of fabric for backing

66" x 78" piece of batting

CUTTING

Cut all strips across the fabric width (cross grain).

From *each* assorted print, cut:

2 strips, 8" x 40"; crosscut into 10 squares, 8" x 8" (80 total)

From the green inner-border fabric, cut:

6 strips, 1¼" x 42"

From the purple outer-border fabric, cut:

7 strips, 6" x 42"

From the binding fabric, cut:

7 strips, 2½" x 45"

Cut Size: 8" x 8"

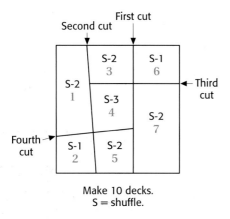

Make 10 decks.
S = shuffle.

Refer to "Making the Blocks, Stack the Deck Style" on page 11 for guidance as needed. These blocks are shuffled using the controlled shuffling technique described on page 14. If you are using a cutting template, use the chipped template technique described on page 12.

1. Arrange the 8" assorted squares into 10 decks of eight squares each, right sides up, alternating the lights and darks. Each deck should contain a different mix of fabrics. Secure each deck with a pin through all the layers.

2. Working with one deck at a time, cut and shuffle the squares as shown in the diagram above. As you go, secure each deck to a piece of paper by pinning through all the layers.

MAKING THE BLOCKS

Referring to "Sewing the Blocks" on page 15 and the diagrams at left and below, sew the shuffled segments for each block together one block at a time as shown; press. Trim the blocks to 6½" x 6½". Make 80.

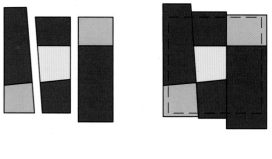

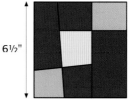

Make 80 blocks.

ASSEMBLING THE QUILT TOP

1. Arrange the blocks into eight vertical rows of 10 blocks each, rotating the blocks as shown in the assembly diagram on page 75. Move the blocks around until you are satisfied with the layout. View your arrangement through a door peephole (see "The 10-Foot Rule" on page 11) to check the color and block balance.

2. Pin and sew the blocks into eight vertical rows; press.

3. Pin and sew the rows from step 2 together in pairs; press.

4. Pin and sew the pairs together; press.

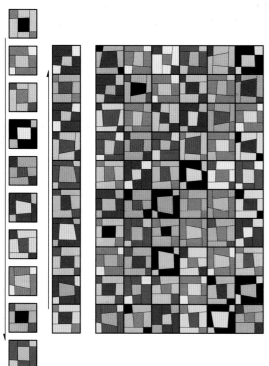

Assembly diagram

ADDING THE BORDERS

1. Refer to "Adding Borders" on page 6. Sew the 1¼"-wide green strips together end to end to make one long inner-border strip.

2. Measure the length of the quilt top through the center and cut two inner-border strips to this measurement. Pin and sew the borders to the sides of the quilt. Press the seams toward the border strips. Measure the width of the quilt top through the center, including the borders just added, and cut two inner-border strips to this measurement. Pin and sew the borders to the top and bottom of the quilt; press.

3. Repeat steps 1 and 2 with the 6"-wide purple outer-border strips to make and attach the outer border.

FINISHING

Refer to "Finishing the Quilt" on page 7 as needed.

1. Divide the backing fabric crosswise into two equal panels, each approximately 67" long. Remove the selvages and sew the pieces together along the long edges to make a backing piece approximately 67" x 80"; press.

2. Layer the quilt top with the batting and backing, keeping the backing seam parallel to the short edges of the quilt top. Baste the layers together using your favorite method.

3. Hand or machine quilt as desired.

4. Trim the backing and batting even with the edges of the quilt top and use the 2½"-wide strips to bind the quilt.

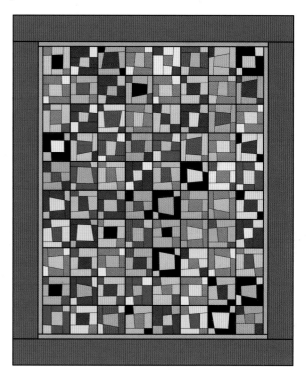

Quilt plan

QUILTING SUGGESTIONS

I quilted in the ditch to anchor the vertical and horizontal seams in the center of the quilt. I quilted diagonally in both directions in the blocks. For the inner border, I quilted in the ditch on the inside seam and added straight-line stitching ¼" from the seam closest to the outer border. I finished with overall stipple quilting in the outer border.

Cherry Preserves

Finished Quilt: 56¼" x 80¾"

Finished Block: 7½" x 7½"

I love the old-fashioned cozy feel of replica prints from the 1930s. I found a batch of different lights printed with sweet little motifs and decided they all needed to be together in a quilt. Cherry appliqués, along with the oversized rickrack, seemed a likely choice for "Cherry Preserves."

FABRIC TIP

I used eight different small-scale 1930s prints with light backgrounds and eight small-scale prints with mixes of red, orange, green, pink, and black. Placing all these prints together in one quilt seemed to make each individual fabric come alive.

MATERIALS

All yardages are based on 42"-wide fabric.

2⅝ yards of yellow fabric for sashing, setting triangles, and border

⅓ yard *each* of 8 assorted red, orange, green, pink, and black 1930s-style prints for blocks

⅓ yard *each* of 8 assorted 1930s-style prints with light backgrounds for blocks

Assorted red scraps for cherries

Assorted green and brown scraps for leaves and branches

¾ yard of fabric for binding

4⅞ yards of fabric for backing

62" x 86" piece of batting

8 yards of 1¾"-wide red rickrack

Removable paper interfacing (optional)

1½ yards of fusible web

CUTTING

Cut all strips across the fabric width (cross grain).

From the assorted red, orange, green, pink, and black 1930s-style prints, cut a *total* of:

20 squares, 9" x 9"

From the assorted 1930s-style prints with light backgrounds, cut a *total* of:

20 squares, 9" x 9"

From the yellow fabric, cut:

14 strips, 1½" x 42"; crosscut 6 strips into 30 strips, 1½" x 8"

2 strips, 13⅜" x 42"; crosscut into 4 squares, 13⅜" x 13⅜". Cut each square diagonally from corner to corner in both directions to yield 4 quarter-square triangles (16 total).

2 squares, 6¼" x 6¼"; cut each square diagonally from corner to corner in one direction to yield 2 half-square triangles (4 total)

7 strips, 5" x 42"

From the binding fabric cut:

8 strips, 2½" x 42"

Block Cutting, Shuffling, and Sewing Guide

Cut Size: 9" x 9"

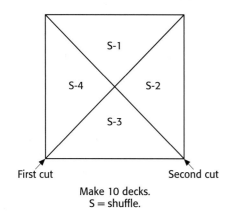

First cut Second cut

Make 10 decks.
S = shuffle.

Refer to "Making the Blocks, Stack the Deck Style" on page 11 for guidance as needed. These blocks are shuffled using the traditional shuffling technique described on page 14. If you are using a cutting template, use the chipped template technique described on page 12.

1. Arrange the 9" assorted colored and light-background squares into 10 decks of four squares each, right sides up, alternating the light-background and colored prints. Each deck should contain a different mix of fabrics. Secure each deck with a pin through all the layers.

2. Working with one deck at a time, cut and shuffle the squares as shown in the diagram above. As you go, secure each deck to a piece of paper by pinning through all the layers.

MAKING THE BLOCKS

Referring to "Sewing the Blocks" on page 15 and the diagram below, sew the shuffled segments for each block together one block at a time as shown. Begin by sewing the segments into pairs; press. Sew the pairs together; press. Trim the blocks to 8" x 8". Make 40.

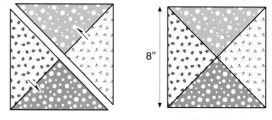

Make 40 blocks.

ASSEMBLING THE QUILT TOP

Refer to "Assembling the Quilt Top" on page 6 for guidance as needed.

1. Sew the 1½" x 42" yellow strips together end to end to make one long sashing strip. Cut the strip into two strips, 25" long; two strips, 42" long; two strips, 59" long; and two strips, 66½" long.

2. Arrange the blocks into nine diagonal rows as shown in the assembly diagram on page 79, leaving room for the sashing. (You will have one block left over. Set it aside for another project.) Move the blocks around and view your arrangement through a door peephole (see "The 10-Foot Rule" on page 11) to check the color and block balance. Once you are happy with the layout, place the 1½" x 8" yellow strips; the assorted 1½"-wide sashing strips from step 1; the yellow quarter-square side, top, and bottom setting triangles; and the yellow half-square corner setting triangles in the layout.

3. Referring to the assembly diagram, pin and sew the blocks and 1½" x 8" strips together to make a row. Press the seams toward the sashing strips. Make seven rows.

4. Pin and sew a 25"-long sashing strip to rows 2 and 8, a 42"-long sashing strip to rows 3 and 7, and a 59"-long sashing strip to rows 4 and 6; press.

5. Sew the yellow top, bottom, and side quarter-square triangles to the rows from step 4 and to the blocks in rows 1 and 9 as shown. Press the seam allowances toward the setting triangles.

6. Sew a side quarter-square triangle to the left edge of row 5 as shown in the assembly diagram; press. Sew a 66"-long sashing strip to the bottom of the row; press. Repeat to sew a side quarter-square triangle to the right edge of row 5 and a 66"-long sashing strip to the top of the row; press.

7. Pin and sew the rows together as follows: rows 1, 2, 3, and 4; and rows 5, 6, 7, 8, and 9. Press the seams to one side.

8. Pin and sew the sections from step 7 together; press.

9. Add the four corner triangles. Press the seams toward the corner triangles.

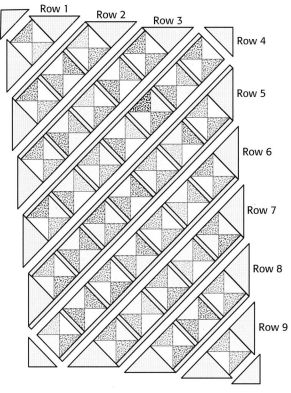

Assembly diagram

ADDING THE BORDERS AND RICKRACK

1. Refer to "Adding Borders" on page 6. Sew the 5"-wide yellow strips together end to end to make one long border strip.

2. Measure the length of the quilt top through the center and cut two border strips to this measurement. Pin and sew the borders to the sides of the quilt. Press the seams toward the border strips. Measure the width of the quilt top through the center, including the borders just added, and cut two border strips to this measurement. Pin and sew the borders to the top and bottom of the quilt; press.

3. Machine baste the rickrack directly over the seams between the body of the quilt and the border.

RICKRACK TRICK

Before adding the rickrack, place removable paper interfacing on the back of the quilt, covering the seams between the quilt and the border. This helps stabilize the quilt as you stitch the rickrack in place.

ADDING THE APPLIQUÉS

1. Referring to "Fusible-Web Appliqué" on page 5, use the patterns on pages 80–81 and the assorted red, green, and brown scraps to prepare the appliqués for four of cherry cluster A and five of cherry cluster B for fusing.

2. Referring to the quilt photo on page 76, position and fuse the prepared appliqués to the quilt top. Use your favorite method to stitch around the outer edges of the shapes. I used a straight stitch just inside the edges.

FINISHING

Refer to "Finishing the Quilt" on page 7 as needed.

1. Divide the backing fabric crosswise into two equal panels, each approximately 88" long. Remove the selvages and sew the pieces together along the long edges to make a backing piece approximately 80" x 88"; press. Trim the backing to 2" to 3" larger than the quilt top all around.

2. Layer the quilt top with the batting and backing, keeping the backing seam parallel to the long edges of the quilt top. Baste the layers together using your favorite method.

3. Hand or machine quilt as desired. Secure the rickrack by quilting just inside each edge.

4. Trim the backing and batting even with the edges of the quilt top and use the 2½"-wide strips to bind the quilt.

Quilt plan

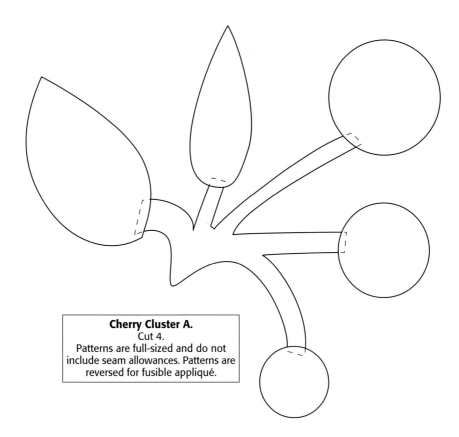

Cherry Cluster A.
Cut 4.
Patterns are full-sized and do not include seam allowances. Patterns are reversed for fusible appliqué.

Cherry Cluster B.
Cut 5.
Patterns are full-sized and do not
include seam allowances. Patterns are
reversed for fusible appliqué.

Catch a Falling Star

Finished Quilt: 44½" x 55½"
Finished Block: 5½" x 5½"

In addition to lots of fabrics, wavy lines are a favorite design element of mine. Once this quilt came together, appliquéd falling stars in three sizes seemed appropriate to accent the light and dark blue skies.

FABRIC TIPS

I chose a variety of dreamy blue prints with small-scale designs for this quilt. Half the fabrics are a dark value and half are a medium value.

MATERIALS

All yardages are based on 42"-wide fabric.

7/8 yard of blue fabric for outer border

1/4 yard *each* of 6 assorted medium blue and 6 assorted dark blue prints for blocks (12 fabrics total)

1/3 yard of purple fabric for inner border

Assorted yellow and gold scraps for stars

1/2 yard of fabric for binding

2 7/8 yards of fabric for backing

50" x 60" piece of batting

3/4 yard of fusible web

CUTTING

Cut all strips across the fabric width (cross grain).

From *each* dark blue print, cut:

1 strip, 7" x 42"; crosscut into 4 rectangles, 7" x 9" (24 total)

From *each* medium blue print, cut:

1 strip, 7" x 42"; crosscut into 4 squares, 7" x 7" (24 total)

From the purple fabric, cut:

5 strips, 1 1/2" x 42"

From the blue outer-border fabric, cut:

5 strips, 5" x 42"

From the binding fabric, cut:

6 strips, 2 1/2" x 42"

Block Cutting, Shuffling, and Sewing Guide

Cut Size: 7" x 9"

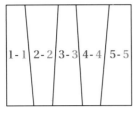

Make 4 decks.

Refer to "Making the Blocks, Stack the Deck Style" on page 11 for guidance as needed. These blocks are shuffled using the traditional shuffling technique described on page 14. If you are using a cutting template, use the whole-segment template technique described on page 12.

1. Arrange the 7" x 9" assorted dark blue rectangles into four decks of six rectangles each, right sides up. Each deck should contain a different mix of fabrics. Secure each deck with a pin through all the layers.

2. Working with one deck at a time, cut and shuffle the pieces as shown in the diagram above. Vary the width and angle of the cuts from deck to deck so that all decks are cut a little differently from one another. As you go, secure each deck to a piece of paper by pinning through all the layers.

MAKING THE BLOCKS

1. Referring to "Sewing the Blocks" on page 15 and the diagrams above and below, sew the shuffled segments for each block together with the chain-piecing technique. Press the seams to one side. Make 24. Trim the blocks to 7" x 7". (It's OK if your blocks are a little smaller; just trim them all to the same size and trim the 7" medium blue squares to match.)

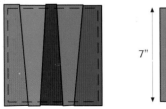

Make 24 blocks.

2. With both right sides up, layer a block from step 1 with a 7" medium blue square. Referring to the tip on page 13 ("Cutting Curves"), cut the block apart diagonally from corner to corner, adding a little curve in the center of the block. Repeat for each block from step 1.

3. Shuffle the segments on one side of the block so that a pieced segment is paired with a medium blue segment. Referring to "Sewing Curves" on page 16, sew the segments together; press. Make 48. Trim the blocks to 6" x 6".

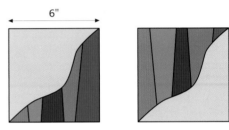

Make 48 total.

ASSEMBLING THE QUILT TOP

Refer to "Assembling the Quilt Top" on page 6 for guidance as needed.

1. Arrange the blocks into six vertical rows of eight blocks each, turning the blocks as shown in the assembly diagram on page 85. Move the blocks around until you are satisfied with the layout. View your arrangement through a door peephole (see "The 10-Foot Rule" on page 11) to check the color and block balance.

2. Pin and sew the blocks together into six vertical rows; press.

3. Pin and sew the rows from step 2 together in pairs; press.

4. Pin and sew the pairs together; press.

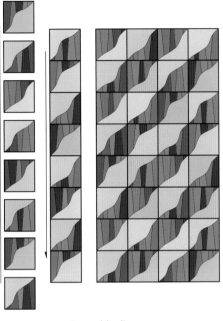

Assembly diagram

ADDING THE BORDERS

1. Refer to "Adding Borders" on page 6. Sew the 1½"-wide purple strips together end to end to make one long inner-border strip.

2. Measure the length of the quilt top through the center and cut two inner-border strips to this measurement. Pin and sew the borders to the sides of the quilt. Press the seams toward the border strips. Measure the width of the quilt top through the center, including the borders just added, and cut two inner-border strips to this measurement. Pin and sew the borders to the top and bottom of the quilt; press.

3. Repeat steps 1 and 2 with the 5"-wide blue outer-border strips to make and attach the outer border.

ADDING THE APPLIQUÉS

1. Referring to "Fusible-Web Appliqué" on page 5, use the patterns on page 86 and the assorted yellow and gold scraps to prepare the appliqués for a total of 12 stars for fusing.

2. Referring to the quilt photo on page 82, position and fuse the prepared appliqués to the quilt top. Use your favorite method to stitch around the outer edges of the shapes. I used a machine blanket stitch and black thread as an accent around the star edges.

FINISHING

Refer to "Finishing the Quilt" on page 7 as needed.

1. Divide the backing fabric crosswise into two equal panels, each approximately 52" long. Remove the selvages and sew the pieces together along the long edges to make a backing piece approximately 52" x 80"; press. Trim the backing to 2" to 3" larger than the quilt top all around.

2. Layer the quilt top with the batting and backing, keeping the backing seam parallel to the short edges of the quilt top. Baste the layers together using your favorite method.

3. Hand or machine quilt as desired.

4. Trim the backing and batting even with the edges of the quilt top and use the 2½"-wide strips to bind the quilt.

Quilt plan

QUILTING SUGGESTIONS

I machine quilted a whimsical stipple pattern over the blocks and outer border. For the inner border, I quilted in the ditch on the inside seam and added straight-line stitching ¼" from the seam closest to the outer border.

Patterns are full-sized and do not
include seam allowances. Patterns are
reversed for fusible appliqué.

Wild Wind

Finished Quilt: 57½" x 78½"
Finished Block: 10½" x 10½"

The autumnlike appearance of this quilt results from a combination of beautiful, deep colors. I combined this palette with an asymmetrical block to create the look of kites or windmills.

FABRIC TIP

I chose a rich, harmonious blend of gold, brown, green, and purple prints. Most of them have a small pattern but appear solid from a distance.

MATERIALS

All yardages are based on 42"-wide fabric.

1½ yards of dark burnt red print for outer border

½ yard *each* of 6 assorted (for example, gold, dark burnt orange, light to medium gold, light olive green, creamy yellow, and light green) prints for blocks

½ yard *each* of 2 different very dark purple prints for blocks

½ yard of dark brown fabric for inner border

⅔ yard of fabric for binding

4¾ yards of fabric for backing

63" x 84" piece of batting

CUTTING

Cut all strips across the fabric width (cross grain).

From *each* assorted print, cut:

1 strip, 12½" x 42"; crosscut into 3 squares, 12½" x 12½" (18 total)

From *each* dark purple print, cut:

1 strip, 12½" x 42"; crosscut into 3 squares, 12½" x 12½" (6 total)

From the dark brown fabric, cut:

6 strips, 2" x 42"

From the dark burnt red print, cut:

7 strips, 6½" x 42"

From the binding fabric, cut:

8 strips, 2½" x 42"

Block Cutting, Shuffling, and Sewing Guide

Cut Size: 12½" x 12½"

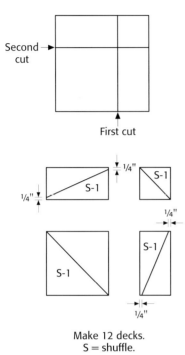

Make 12 decks.
S = shuffle.

Refer to "Making the Blocks, Stack the Deck Style" on page 11 for guidance as needed. These blocks are shuffled using the controlled shuffling technique described on page 14. If you are using a cutting template, use the chipped template technique described on page 12.

1. Arrange the 12½" assorted-print and purple squares into 12 decks of two squares each, right sides up, alternating the lights and darks. Each deck should contain a different mix of fabrics. Secure each deck with a pin through all the layers.

2. Working with one deck at a time, cut and shuffle the squares as shown in the diagrams above. As you go, secure each deck to a piece of paper by pinning through all the layers.

MAKING THE BLOCKS

Referring to "Sewing the Blocks" on page 15 and the diagrams at left and below, sew the shuffled segments for each block together one block at a time; press. Trim the blocks to 10½" x 10½". Make 24 blocks total; 12 each of block A and block B.

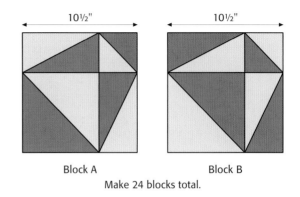

Block A   Block B
Make 24 blocks total.

ASSEMBLING THE QUILT TOP

Refer to "Assembling the Quilt Top" on page 6 for guidance as needed. You might find it helpful to separate the blocks into two stacks before you begin laying out the quilt. Place all the A blocks in one stack and all the B blocks in the other stack.

1. Arrange the blocks into six *horizontal* rows of four blocks each, paying careful attention to the positioning of the blocks as shown in the assembly diagram on page 90. The blocks in rows 1, 3, and 5 are identically positioned A blocks. The blocks in rows 2, 4, and 6 are identically positioned B blocks. View your arrangement through a door peephole (see "The 10-Foot Rule" on page 11) to check the color and block balance.

2. Pin and sew the blocks into six horizontal rows; press.

3. Pin and sew the rows from step 2 together in pairs; press.

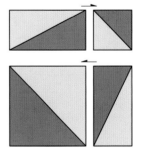

4. Pin and sew the pairs together; press.

Assembly diagram

ADDING THE BORDERS

1. Refer to "Adding Borders" on page 6. Sew the 2"-wide brown strips together end to end to make one long inner-border strip.

2. Measure the length of the quilt top through the center and cut two inner-border strips to this measurement. Pin and sew the borders to the sides of the quilt. Press the seams toward the border strips. Measure the width of the quilt top through the center, including the borders just added, and cut two inner-border strips to this measurement. Pin and sew the borders to the top and bottom of the quilt; press.

3. Repeat steps 1 and 2 with the 6½"-wide red strips to make and attach the outer border.

FINISHING

Refer to "Finishing the Quilt" on page 7 as needed.

1. Divide the backing fabric crosswise into two equal panels, each approximately 85" long. Remove the selvages and sew the pieces together along the long edges to make a backing piece approximately

80" x 85"; press. Trim the backing to 2" to 3" larger than the quilt top all around.

2. Layer the quilt top with the batting and backing, keeping the backing seam parallel to the long edges of the quilt top. Baste the layers together using your favorite method.

3. Hand or machine quilt as desired.

4. Trim the backing and batting even with the edges of the quilt top and use the 2½"-wide strips to bind the quilt.

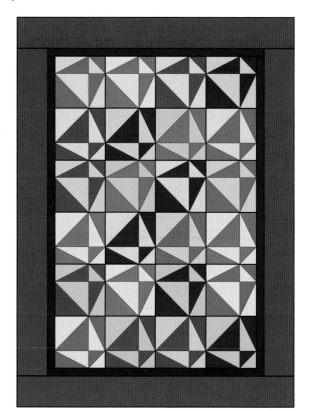

Quilt plan

QUILTING SUGGESTIONS

I machine stitched in the ditch of each seam in the blocks and in the vertical and horizontal seams between the blocks. For the inner border, I quilted in the ditch on the inside seam and added straight-line stitching ¼" from the seam closest to the outer border. I finished with overall stipple quilting in the outer border.

Finished Quilt: 49½" x 67½"

Finished Block: 6" x 6"

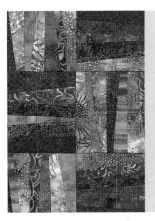

This quilt was inspired by watching the changing seasons through my studio windows. Spring and summer are always filled with beautifully colored flowers and budding trees. When fall arrives, the already-beautiful colors take on a new look, mixing the bright flowers in with the falling leaves. "Summer's End" is a result of this view.

FABRIC TIPS

For the blocks, I chose a group of medium- to dark-value reds and a group of mostly medium-value blue and turquoises with a few dark values sprinkled in. Most of the prints are batiks.

MATERIALS

All yardages are based on 42"-wide fabric.

1⅛ yards of blue batik for outer border

½ yard of light blue fabric for inner border

⅓ yard *each* of 8 assorted red and 8 assorted blue fabrics for blocks (16 fabrics total)

Assorted red, gold, and brown scraps for leaves

⅝ yard of fabric for binding

3⅛ yards of fabric for backing

55" x 73" piece of batting

¾ yard of fusible web

CUTTING

Cut all strips across the fabric width (cross grain).

From *each* red and blue fabric for blocks, cut:

1 strip, 7¼" x 42"; crosscut into 4 rectangles, 7¼" x 10" (64 total; you will use 56)

From the light blue inner-border fabric, cut:

6 strips, 2" x 42"

From the blue batik, cut:

6 strips, 5½" x 42"

From the binding fabric, cut:

7 strips, 2½" x 42"

Block Cutting, Shuffling, and Sewing Guide

Cut Size: 7¼" x 10"

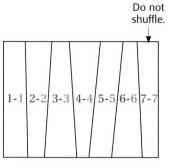

Make 4 decks of each color.

Refer to "Making the Blocks, Stack the Deck Style" on page 11 for guidance as needed. These blocks are shuffled using the traditional shuffling technique described on page 14. If you are using a cutting template, use the whole-segment template technique described on page 12.

1. Arrange the 7¼" x 10" assorted red rectangles into four decks of seven rectangles each, right sides up. Each deck should contain a different mix of fabrics. Secure each deck with a pin through all the layers. Repeat with the assorted blue fabrics.

2. Working with one deck at a time, cut and shuffle the pieces as shown in the diagram above. Vary the width and angle of the cuts from deck to deck so that all decks are cut a little differently from one another. As you go, secure each deck to a piece of paper by pinning through all the layers.

MAKING THE BLOCKS

Referring to "Sewing the Blocks" on page 15 and the diagrams below and at left, sew the shuffled segments for each block together with the chain-piecing technique. Press the seams to one side. Make 28 red blocks and 28 blue blocks. Trim the blocks to 6½" x 6½". (It's OK if your blocks are a little larger or smaller; just trim them all to the same size.)

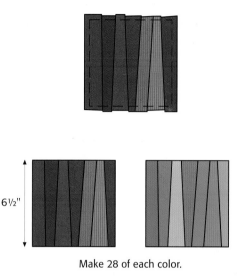

Make 28 of each color.

ASSEMBLING THE QUILT TOP

Refer to "Assembling the Quilt Top" on page 6 for guidance as needed.

1. Arrange the blocks into six vertical rows of nine blocks each, alternating the red and the blue blocks as shown in the assembly diagram on page 94. (You will have one block of each color left over. Set these aside for another project.) Place the red blocks so that the seams run horizontally and the blue blocks so that the seams run vertically. View your arrangement through a door peephole (see "The 10-Foot Rule" on page 11) to check the color and block balance.

2. Pin and sew the blocks together into six vertical rows; press.

3. Pin and sew the rows from step 3 together in pairs; press.

4. Pin and sew the pairs together; press.

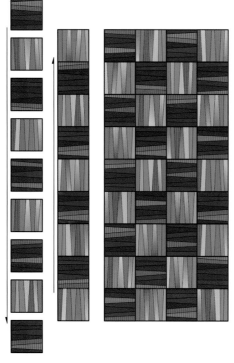

Assembly diagram

ADDING BORDERS

1. Refer to "Adding Borders" on page 6. Sew the 2"-wide light blue strips together end to end to make one long strip.

2. Measure the length of the quilt top through the center and cut two inner-border strips to this measurement. Pin and sew the borders to the sides of the quilt. Press the seams toward the border strips. Measure the width of the quilt top through the center, including the borders just added, and cut two inner-border strips to this measurement. Pin and sew the borders to the top and bottom of the quilt; press.

3. Repeat with the 5½"-wide blue strips to make and attach the outer border.

ADDING THE APPLIQUÉS

1. Referring to "Fusible-Web Appliqué" on page 5, use the patterns on page 95 and the assorted red, gold, and brown scraps to prepare the appliqués for a total of 11 leaves for fusing.

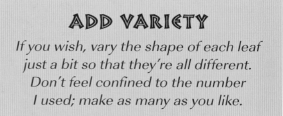

ADD VARIETY

If you wish, vary the shape of each leaf just a bit so that they're all different. Don't feel confined to the number I used; make as many as you like.

2. Referring to the quilt photo on page 91, position and fuse the prepared appliqués to the quilt top. Use your favorite method to stitch around the outer edges of the shapes. I used a straight stitch just inside the cut edges, and then I free-form stitched the veins in the leaves.

FINISHING

Refer to "Finishing the Quilt" on page 7 as needed.

1. Divide the backing fabric crosswise into two equal panels, each approximately 56" long. Remove the selvages and sew the pieces together along the long edges to make a backing piece approximately 56" x 80"; press.

2. Layer the quilt top with the batting and backing, keeping the backing seam parallel to the short edges of the quilt top. Baste the layers together using your favorite method.

3. Hand or machine quilt as desired.

4. Trim the backing and batting even with the edges of the quilt top and use the 2½"-wide strips to bind the quilt.

QUILTING SUGGESTIONS

I used the straight stitch on my machine to quilt a 3"-square grid over the blocks. For the inner border, I quilted in the ditch on the inside seam and added straight-line stitching ¼" from the seam closest to the outer border. I finished with overall stipple quilting in the outer border.

Patterns are full-sized and do not include seam allowances. Patterns are reversed for fusible appliqué.

About the Author

Karla Alexander has been making quilts in a traditional style for cribs and family beds since she was a young girl. However, within the last ten years or so, she began exploring the possibilities of quilting and developing her own quiltmaking style and methods. Teaching at local quilt shops encouraged her to design, publish, and present her own patterns and techniques. As a result, she founded Saginaw Street Quilt Company in the fall of 1998. Today she continues to self-publish an ever-increasing and diverse pattern line.

Introducing Saginaw Street Quilt Company to the world at International Quilt Market in Houston, Texas, in October of 2001 was an enormous step for Karla, and it provided her with the inspiration to write her first book, *Stack the Deck!* It's a book about quick and easy methods for Crazy quilts and was published by Martingale & Company in 2002. Her second book, *Stack a New Deck* (Martingale & Company), made its appearance in 2004 and put her techniques to work without the Crazy quilt look. *New Cuts for New Quilts* is her third book and melds her stacking, cutting, and sewing techniques with traditional as well as unusual designs.

A significant part of Karla's life is spent teaching others to embrace the world of quiltmaking. Traveling and immersing herself in the education of creative quilters has become a learning experience for her. Karla's books and teaching style encourage visual play—endless variations of arrangements without any preconceived notions of the end result. In her opinion, predetermining results sets limitations on individuality. Her quilt designs are simply the starting point for another's inspiration. In Karla's classes, students are given the freedom to break traditional patchwork rules and discover and trust their own capabilities. As she celebrates the publication of her third book, Karla is looking ahead to dreams of fresh designs and taking time to meet and enjoy new students and travels.